Praise for *Would Moses Throw a Chair?*

Storytellers reveal their stories. But, in the case of *Would Moses Throw a Chair?*, the stories reveal the storyteller as an authentic voice with wide-ranging tales and a commitment to finding the bigger message in both the grandiose and the mundane.

—Martha N. Johnson
Author and Former Administrator
U.S. General Services Administration

A husband, father, son, soldier, minister, teacher, and university president, Randall O'Brien shares stories from an abundant and diverse life. Some will make you laugh, some may make you cry, but all will reveal life's lessons from a man with a loving heart, sharp wit, and a deep and abiding faith. His plain spoken style makes for an easy read but belies the depth and import of the many enlightening messages conveyed in his stories. Enjoy the journey.

—Major General Michael Jones
U.S. Army (Ret.)

A warm invitation into the memories and meditations of an accomplished leader, academic, and minister. *Would Moses Throw a Chair?* is both deep and down-to-earth. Through his life's most humorous and stirring experiences, Randall explores the human condition and calls us to greater love for one another.

—Linda A. Livingstone, PhD
Baylor University President

If you are fortunate enough to know Dr. O'Brien, you hear his voice in every word of these stories. He writes as he speaks, a Mississippi-intoned narrative that draws you into the paths he walks and the people he meets, from the jungles of Vietnam, to an Arkansas pulpit, to a honky-tonk in Mississippi. So, pour yourself a glass of sweet tea, sit back, and enjoy—and you might just learn something along the way.

—David Z. Nowell
President, Hope Institute
Author, Dirty Faith

No one tells a story quite like Randall O'Brien—and it helps that (most of) his stories are true. This collection of flash-nonfiction is like having Dr. O'Brien over for a long, wonderful meal.

—Mark Osler
Robert and Marion Short Distinguished Professor of Law
University of St. Thomas (MN)

I can hear Randall's voice as I read these wonderful mini stories! You'll laugh, you'll cry, and you'll ponder the deeper issues as life as you read through this delightful collection of personal narratives. Every time you spend a moment with Randall you'll be guaranteed to hear a thoughtful account that will leave you with a smile on your face and a desire to become a better person. I'm so encouraged that Randall has taken the time and effort to capture these stories in written form to be shared with generations to come. Grab a sweet tea, find a comfortable place to sit, and get ready for an enjoyable read!

—Dr. Claude Pressnell, Jr.
President
Tennessee Independent Colleges and Universities Association

While many readers of this book will have heard J. Randall O'Brien tell a story . . . or two, there will be others who have yet to have the privilege and joy of hearing this Pastor-Preacher-Professor-Provost-President spin a yarn. All who read the stories in *Would Moses Throw a Chair?*, however, will hear the heart and see the soul of a master storyteller, and in so doing, you will laugh and cry even as you ponder and wonder why stories, especially his stories, are so meaningful and powerful. Then, along with me, you will ask, just as we did when we were kids, why story-time (with Randall) had to end so soon.

—Todd D. Still, Ph.D.
Charles J. and Eleanor McLerran DeLancey Dean &
William M. Hinson Professor of Christian Scriptures
Baylor University, Truett Seminary

Randall O'Brien is someone who sees the world in parable. In this collection of stories, we have the opportunity to look through his eyes and glimpse the extraordinary presence of God in some of the ordinary moments of his life (and a few extraordinary moments, as well). After reading this book, you may notice God at work in your own life, in ways and in places you never considered.

—Dr. Robert E. Wallace
Senior Pastor, McLean Baptist Church
McLean, Virginia

Ken Chaffin said, "God had one Son. He made Him a preacher. And He told stories." Stories lie at the heart of the human experience and Randall O'Brien is one of the great encouragers and storytellers of our time. He is the king of the life parable. He sneaks truth in by the side door and opens the reader to a bigger, brighter God-filled world. Do yourself a favor and spend some time in these pages.

—Steve Wells, DMin
Pastor of South Main Baptist Church
Houston, Texas

Smyth & Helwys Publishing, Inc.
6316 Peake Road
Macon, Georgia 31210-3960
1-800-747-3016

Photography by Ricke Hester

Library of Congress Cataloging-in-Publication Data
Names: O'Brien, Randall, author.
Title: Would Moses throw a chair? : stories from the journey / by James Randall O'Brien.
Description: Macon, GA : Smyth & Helwys Publishing, 2021. | Includes bibliographical references.
Identifiers: LCCN 2021040577 | ISBN 9781641733328 (paperback)
Subjects: LCSH: O'Brien, Randall--Anecdotes. | Baptists--Clergy--Biography.
Classification: LCC BX6495.O28 A3 2021 | DDC 286/.1092 [B]--dc23/eng/20211130
LC record available at https://lccn.loc.gov/2021040577

WOULD MOSES THROW A CHAIR?

Stories from the Journey

JAMES RANDALL O'BRIEN

Also by James Randall O'Brien

Set Free by Forgiveness

I Feel Better All Over Than I Do Anywhere Else

Slow Train A'comin', Fast One A'goin':
The Life and Times of James Randall O'Brien
(privately published)

Dedication

To the Master Storyteller

Contents

Introduction 1

Love

A Young Boy, a Blind Dog, and an Old Fool 7
Adam Finds His Rib 9
Baby's Best Friend 11
Eucharist of Beer and Pretzel 13
Inasmuch 17
Jonah 4:7 19
Man's Best Friend 21
No Bull 23
Schoolboy Memories of Schoolgirl Moments 25
Unforgettable Allison Dickson 27

Hypocrisy

Giving Christ a Black Eye 31
Looking Glass 33
Stealing Credit 35
The Gold-embossed Funeral Invitation 37
The Least Understood of All God's Commandments 39

Forgiveness

Did Moses Ever Throw a Chair? 43
Forgiveness for Foolin' Around 45
Now I Know How John the Baptist Felt 49
I Confessed My Sin to Billy Graham 51
Well, I'll Be Doggone, but He Wasn't 53

Race

A Black Pastor, a White Deacon, and a New Day 57
Bronze Star for Brenda 61
Love Wins 65
Pilgrim in a Racist Land 67
With Liberty and Justice for All 77

Musings

Failure and Other Blessings 83
Getting Leah 87
Joy to the World of Insects and Humans 89
Mabel's Beauty Shop & Chain Saw Repair 91
Miss America Dreamin' in Vietnam 93
Running Bare 95
Sisyphus and the Peasant 97
What's It All About, Alfie? 99
Why Evil, Ponders a Five-year-old Child 103

Gratitude

A Leper in Waco 107
An Unexpected Blessing 109
I Once Had a Friend 111
Knowing a Great Deal When I Hear One 113
Records Are Made to Be Corrected 115

Hard Times

Charlie's Pen and Pencil Set 121
Dumb, Dumber, Dumbest 123
I Filled Up the Bag in the Airplane 125
Let's Give It Another Shot 127
Momma Said There'd Be Days Like This 129
This Ability or Disability 133
Wally Christian's Twelve-foot Pole 135

Death

Buck Gibson Survives Hell 139
Hot LZs 141

Learning the Rest of the Story Fifty Years Later 143
Life or Death in Vietnam 147
Not Again? 151
Paying the Price 153
"Playing Chicken" versus Eating Chicken 155
The Day the Taliban Turned Around 157
The Moral of Jimmy's Story 161

Redemption
A Hard Head and a Concrete Court 165
A Killer Gets Life 169
All's Well That Ends Well 171
Fishin' for Men 175
The Rain of a King 177

Surprise
A Snake Named Jake 183
The Amazing Grace of Dr. Oseola McCarty 187
Angels' Wings Spotted 189
Dining on Musgoes 191
Have I Got a Sweater for YOU 195
Oh, Chute! Am I Jumping out of a Perfectly Good Airplane? 195
A Sputnik and a Surprise 199
Tennis, Anyone? 201
The Case of the Illegally Cut and Stolen Christmas Tree 203
The Weirdest Liquid on Earth 207
What Kris Learned from His Father 209
When Dreams Come True 211

Introduction

Why do we tell stories? Why do we listen to them? Why do we enjoy them? We may just as well ask, "Why do we eat, drink, and breathe?" Storytelling is innate to the human experience. "God made man," Nobel laureate Elie Wiesel writes, "because He loves stories."[1] We might add, "And He created us in His image!"

Everyone loves a good story. Not surprisingly, the Good Book, the world's best-selling volume, is a storybook. Filling its pages are epics of creation, the first family, humankind's fall into sin, redemption, the coming of a Savior, the end times, and a new creation. Human life is also a storybook, containing sequels within stories and even other narratives within those tales. We are all connected through our stories. We all breathe. We all bleed. We all love. We all die.

Stories break life's encrypted code: "All we need is love. Love is all we need." Four young mop-top troubadours known as the Beatles crooned our secret. Yet are we not all troubadours in some way? Balladeers living our ballads? Serenaders and serenaded alike, embracing our serenade?

My collection of tales from travels in Russia, war in Vietnam, and places we have lived in Mississippi, Louisiana, Arkansas, Connecticut, Texas, Tennessee, and Iowa speak to and for all of us. We're all in this together, connected by our stories.

Every story is sacred. Word is sacrament. Our presence lies within. So does the Eternal. Stories are burning bushes from which God speaks. As Elizabeth Barrett Browning puts it, "Earth's crammed with Heaven / And every common bush afire with God; / But only

---

1. From *Gates of the Forest* (New York: Holt, Rinehart, and Winston, 1966), 12.

he who sees, takes off his shoes, / The rest sit round it and pluck blackberries."[2]

And this reminds me of a story.

Once there was a man who could neither talk nor walk. His life was a mystery to all, since as a young boy he would sing merrily and dance. As he grew older, however, he became a loner, leaving family and society and choosing to live alone outside the village, where he was fed by birds.

One day a young maiden skipped along the path winding by the hermit's hut. Seeing the poor man, she stopped and asked, "Why do you look so sad?" He did not answer. "If you walk with me among the field and flowers," she said, "you will find your smile." The man did not move.

The maiden sat down beside the loner and began to tell a story. As she weaved her yarn, the man listened intently. Then she suddenly stopped and rose to leave. "Don't go," pleaded the man. "The story you tell is mine. How did you know?"

Saying nothing, the girl continued to walk away. "Please," said the hermit, rising to follow the young maiden. "How did you know?"

"Dance with me," invited the girl.

"But I cannot dance," said the man.

"Your answer awaits you at the end of the dance," she replied.

The curious man began to dance with the fair maiden. Swinging around, they talked delightfully, laughing, until he announced, "I can talk and walk!"

"Of course, you can," said the girl. "And dance!"

"But your story. You were telling my story. How did you know? And how does it end?"

"There is no end," replied the girl, "like a river flowing to the sea. Together we round a bend. Others await. I must go now," she said.

"No, wait! Please tell me how you know my story," he begged.

"Because the story belongs to all of us," she said. "We all struggle with loneliness, with togetherness. Without each other we slowly die.

---

2. From *Aurora Leigh* (World's Classics; New York: Oxford University Press, 1993), Book VII, ll. 821–23.

With each other, we sing and dance, grieve and hope, dream and live. Share the story with others, as I have with you, and you will live!"

LOVE

A Young Boy, a Blind Dog, and an Old Fool

Katie Belle and Christopher were born the same year. One in April, the other in September. Both in 1988. One's a girl, the other one's a boy. Christopher (who now goes by Kris) is our son; Katie Belle is our cocker spaniel.

Christopher is growing up. Katie Belle is growing old. I remember potty training both of them. Feeding them, bathing them, playing with them, cleaning up after them. They're close, those two. Once I saw them sitting on the back step sharing the same biscuit.

While Kris is growing strong, Katie is growing weak. Dog years are taking their toll. Katie is heavy now, slow, no longer slim nor frisky. She is tired, blind, deaf. Sleeps a lot. One day, someday, will be a hard day, if you know what I mean.

Lately, I've been preparing myself psychologically for that time. "She's so pitiful, bless her heart. One day she'll be outta her misery."

Thursday evening, July 11, 1996, the entire family piles into the car, rushing to Kris's baseball game. In a mad hurry. Can't be late. I'm the coach. I back over something in the drive. I look and see nothing. Head out the drive. Kay looks back, sees Katie Belle limping wildly in blind circles. "Hon, you've run over Katie Belle!"

What to do? Game won't wait. Starts in fifteen minutes. I'm the coach. Poor Katie! Kay and the girls rush Katie to the vet in our other car. Kris and I speed to the ballpark.

Katie's hip is knocked out of joint. Nothing broken, thank goodness. Emergency vet bill is $200. Surgery to ensure the hip remains in place would be an additional $600. We're all upset about poor Katie's injuries. I feel horrible. "How could I not see her? I'm so sorry, kids."

I should be honest. I'm also feeling fairly sick over the dollar loss. By the second day I'm lamenting aloud. "Can't believe how much my carelessness is going to cost me. Nearly $1,000! Poor blind dog. Even if she can't see, can't she hear and get out of the way?"

"Dad!"

"I know, I know. But the vet said the surgery might not even fix the leg. I sure hate spending that much money on an uncertainty."

Silence. Whole family. Forever. Then seven-year-old Kris breaks the silence. "Daddy, you love Katie Belle more than you do your money, don't you?"

". . . and a little child shall lead them."

Adam Finds His Rib

"And the rib, which the LORD God had taken from the man, made he a woman, and brought her unto the man." (Genesis 2:22, KJV)

I'm sitting in the college cafeteria feeling sorry for myself. After returning home from Vietnam, trying out as a walk-on punter for the Tennessee Volunteers, and making the team, I am supposed to be in Knoxville enrolling in the University of Tennessee this semester. Reluctantly giving in to my longtime girlfriend's months-long pleas to matriculate at her university, however, I have passed up my dream to kick for the Vols and instead enrolled in-state.

Here is the kicker (pun intended): after shelling out thousands of dollars in private university tuition, I am stuck in Mississippi at a strange school when she breaks up with me and attends another college. My immediate attempts to secure a tuition refund are denied; the refund deadline has passed. Try as I might—with her or with the school—nothing changes.

So here I sit depressed.

And I look and behold, a door is opened in heaven. And the voice I hear is like a trumpet speaking. "Look hither! I will show you new and beautiful things which must come to pass hereafter." Immediately, I turn and see an angel—brown-eyed, brunette, shapely, clothed with the sun, stars sparkling in her hair, gliding on air down our cafeteria aisle. And a voice like many waters sounds from heaven saying, "Prettier than a football, isn't she?"

I never transfer.

And the rib, which the LORD God had taken from the man, made he a woman, and brought her to the man. And Adam exclaimed, "Now!

This is bone of my bone and flesh of my flesh!" Which, being translated, means, "HOT DIGGITY DOG!"

"Would you like to meet her?" asks the guy sitting at my table. "That's Kay Donahoe, one of my friends."

And some say it thundered!

"Randall, this is Kay Donahoe."

"Hi." My puberty-like, breaking voice cracks.

"Kay, this is Randall O'Brien."

"I love you." Now, to this day, she says she said, "How are you?" But I think we know better, don't we?

The next time I see Kay on campus, she's walking to class. Ever so discreetly, crossing over to her side of the street, walking nonchalantly toward her, I say, "Hi, Kay."

"Hi, Bruce."

Bruce? Some impression I make.

(Historical footnote: Three years later, Kay accepts the opportunity to walk down the aisle [yes, our children and grandchildren love this story] and repeat to yours truly the words she denies whispering the day God brought Adam his rib.)

Baby's Best Friend

Man's best friend.

Dogs have long been called our best pals. In the adage, "man," of course, refers to mankind, humankind, all of us—not just males.

Stories abound of furry heroes protecting loved ones. Science has even rendered evidence that canine companionship elevates human levels of serotonin and dopamine, those "feel good" chemicals secreted by our brains. Now, if it's "feel good" you want, try this:

Infant abandonment is a problem in Kenya, where poverty and underage pregnancy often combine so that a young mother feels helpless to care for her newborn baby. Authorities report that the Ngong Forest near the nation's capital of Nairobi tragically provides a dumping ground for unwanted newborn infants.

One such abandoned baby fell into the paws of a life-saving friend. A stray mother dog with her own litter of pups apparently heard the cries of the abandoned infant while foraging in the forest for food. No one knows the full story, but the baby wrapped in a bag was found nestled within the litter of puppies behind a shed across the highway from the forest. The stray canine mother, it appears, found the infant in the sack, carried the bag in her teeth across the busy highway, and placed the child among her own pups.

Aggrey Mwalimu, owner of the shed, shared that the baby was discovered after two children heard cries coming from the area of the shed. A tan and white mixed-breed dog was found lying protectively beside the baby. The children's mother removed the infant and gave him a bath, milk, and fresh clothes. Then she took him to the police station. Soon the baby was in the care of hospital personnel. Reported to be responding well to treatment, including antibiotics to treat an infected umbilical cord, the infant named "Angel" by hospital staff appeared to be doing well.

The name given the young seven-pound, four-ounce survivor seems to be a nice fit. At the same time, our nameless heroic canine rescuer, herself an abandoned furry sweetheart, deserves a name as well. "Baby's Best Friend" may be a little awkward for a name. But history offers a thousand proofs, including one in Kenya, that there's always room for one more "Angel."[3]

---

3. Associated Press, "Stray Dog Saves Life of Abandoned Baby," May 10, 2005, https://www.nbcnews.com/health/health-news/stray-dog-saves-life-abandoned-baby-flna1c9443048.

Eucharist of Beer and Pretzel

Sometimes we long to receive what we refuse to give.

Dad drank. Nothing unusual about that. Irish men, though, may be prone to overdoing it. Family members of problem drinkers often don't get much of what they need. Sometimes it's milk, sometimes supper, sometimes a winter coat. Sometimes it's a trip to the dentist, shoes, or a good night's sleep. Sometimes it's hugs, kisses, attention, worship together as a family.

When a child grows up playing second fiddle to a can of beer or a bottle of whiskey, they unconsciously begin to try hard to earn attention and favor. Competition with the bottle becomes a way of life. Unconditional love and acceptance from the alcoholic parent may be lacking, or may seem to be, since the parent's apparent pleasure is the drug and not the child. Childhood vows of abstinence and family devotion form often in alcoholic homes.

In giving my life to Christian ministry, I confess I had hoped to save the world, especially my own family.

Now for the story.

One of my nephews was getting married. When my nephew's wedding date arrived, our family traveled ten hours for the joyful occasion. The ceremony was beautiful; the weather was horrible. A torrential downpour baptized all of us as we darted from the church to our car to travel to the reception hall miles away.

We arrived at the reception to find the party in full swing, beer and hard liquor flowing like white-capping rivers. Three lines formed: the beer line, the liquor line, and the food line. It seemed like everyone was drinking and smoking wholeheartedly. Even the bride, standing in the center of the ballroom in her sparkling, sequined white gown, held in her hand a clear plastic cup full of golden beer topped with thick, white foam.

As the wedding party, guests, and relatives danced and imbibed well into the night, first I grew irritable, then sick to my stomach. The forced march down memory lane beat me up emotionally. Dad sat drinking heavily with the others. I hated it all, every minute of it!

"Are y'all ready to go?" I finally demanded in disgust. Kay, our three children (ages seventeen, fifteen, ten), my sisters, and Mother and Daddy looked at me in shock. Surely we had not driven ten hours simply to pay our respects and then race home! So Kay reasoned, "Hon, why don't you get something else to eat so we can visit a little while longer? We're not in a rush."

I stamped away agitated. Prowling outside the hall, I planted myself on the small front porch and eyed the deluge, feeling like an alien. Ten, fifteen minutes passed; my pain did not. I stalked back inside. "Look, I'm leaving. You can ride with me, or ride back to the hotel with somebody else."

Giving in to my anger, my parents and family rose to leave with me. As we drove home cold and drenched from the downpour, no one said a word. Miles down the road a red and blue neon sign in the window of a Louisiana honky-tonk, advertising cold beer, pierced the dark, stormy night. Through the ocean of water flooding our overwhelmed windshield wipers, Dad spied the sign.

"Pull in there! I want a beer."

"Donald, you don't need another beer," Mother tried.

"I can have a beer if I want one, dammit!"

What to do? Mother and I had fought on this hill for endless years. Nightmares haunt too long. I steered the SUV into the gravel parking lot of the ill-lit dive. Our children had not trod this path. With wind-blown, horizontal rain pelting our vehicle in blinding sheets, Dad's diminished physical condition due to twenty years of Parkinson's disease left him a cruel target for the unrelenting storm. So I barked, "What do you want?"

"Budweiser."

Into the tempest I dashed. Entering the dimly lit beer joint, I ordered at the bar and then returned soaked with Dad's addiction. I handed it to him, along with a pretzel. No one said a word.

Next day, the trip home was unusually muted. Ten-hour drives pass slowly when no one speaks. Days later, back home, Kay said, "Your son [ten] is asking his sisters why you bought PaPaw beer."

"What are they telling him?"

"I think they don't know what to think."

"Well, I think it's time for a family counsel," I announced.

Gathering the family, we all sat down quietly. I began slowly, "Mother tells me you have some questions about me buying PaPaw beer the other night."

"Well, why did you?"

"Yeah, why did you do that, Dad?"

"How could you do that in front of your son?"

All three kids launched rapid-fire questions. "We can't believe you bought beer, Dad. Why did you do that?"

"I'm gonna tell you kids something that you might not understand—not now, at least. Maybe one day you will. I bought PaPaw beer because I was sick and needed to become well. I was blind and needed to see. I was a hypocrite and tired, tired of craving from Dad what I refused to give him: grace, acceptance, unconditional love.

"See these hands? You've seen these hands serve bread and wine to hundreds of people in church for Communion, or Eucharist as some call it, which means 'good grace.' But until the other night, you've never seen these hands serve a beer to anyone, have you? I want you to remember that night. Because one day you might look back on it and ponder, 'You know that beer and pretzel Daddy handed PaPaw that stormy night in Louisiana sure looks a lot like bread and wine, in reflection.'

"Remember that night. Because I will. It might just be that your Daddy and Papaw went to church together that night for the first time."

Inasmuch

In 1950, Jack Zenk was removed from his home and placed in an orphanage. So the nine-year-old boy pedaled the sixty-five miles back home on his bicycle. Sleeping under a bridge and slipping into the house for food, he managed to be near Ralph and Doris Wagner, the couple he called Mom and Dad.

The Wagners had been his foster parents, but that didn't matter to Jack. Just as it hasn't mattered to 977 other foster children who have called the Wagners Mom and Dad since 1950.

For nearly forty years the Wagners "have taken kids no one wants," says David Klasing, director of McHenry County Court (Illinois) Services. "They try to take each one and let him know he is an individual, someone special. They have a love and concern for the child no matter who he is."

The Wagners have proudly given their daughters away at the altar and anxiously taken countless sons to court. They have put out fires in their home, replaced TV sets blown out by kids playing with the controls, sanded out initials carved into dressers, and sweated through a nightmare when a foster teen gave one of their young daughters a hallucinogenic drug.

Yet, says Doris Wagner, now sixty, "Everybody needs to know you care. We have to make a success of their lives, give them a positive self-image. They respond so much to love, even just a pat on the back. There are some sad times," admits Doris. "But I know every child who has been here has touched our lives for the better."

Jack Zenk, now forty-six, works in Fort Lauderdale, Florida, but he calls the Wagners once a week. "I had lost trust in people, but I trusted them. They straightened me out and taught me to respect people," he says. "You couldn't find any better parents."

Recently, 486 of the foster children and their families went back "home" for a family reunion. In addition to the 486, an approving unseen guest was present. How do I know so much? Oh, I know, all right. I read his words once: *"Inasmuch as you have done it unto the least of these, you have done it unto me."*

Jonah 4:7

"Where did you eat your first honeymoon meal?" When your wedding is in New Orleans, Louisiana, home of some of America's finest cuisine, this question doesn't seem so bizarre.

Chuck Kelley and I are studying on the top floor of the New Orleans seminary library when I pose the question.

"McDonald's," he replies.

"McDonald's! You've *got* to be kidding!"

"I'm not kidding."

"Not Commander's Palace?"

"Goodness! Who can afford Commander's Palace? We were driving out of town. Both of us were starving. You know how it is at receptions. No time to eat. So we pulled into McDonald's. Got a couple of Big Macs, fries, and Cokes. Sure hit the spot!"

"McDonald's? Rhonda must love you."

"We had a great time. Ate. Laughed. Got a napkin and numbered to ten. Made a list of things we want to do in our marriage."

"Now, that's a great idea!"

"Yeah, we've already crossed off a couple of things on the list, too."

"Really? What you gonna do when you cross 'em all off?"

"Go get another McDonald's napkin."

Don't you love it?

A few days later, Chuck and I find ourselves in the library again. "Hey, Chuck, what's your favorite verse in the Bible?"

"Jonah 4:7"

"Jonah 4:7?"

"Yep. Jonah 4:7."

"That's a new one. You might have to help me there. What's Jonah 4:7?"

"*And God appointed a worm.*" He laughed. "I figure if God can use a worm, maybe He can use me, too."

(Historical footnote: The Reverend Dr. Charles "Chuck" Kelley was elected the eighth president of the New Orleans Baptist Theological Seminary in 1996, serving until 2019, when he retired and was named president emeritus.)

Man's Best Friend

A twelve-year-old boy is alive today because of a dog. Greg Holzworth went for a walk in the woods but found himself in trouble when snow, rapidly falling, began covering his tracks.

Wearing only a denim jacket over a t-shirt, Greg fought for his life as an angry storm dumped eight inches of snow on the area and temperatures plunged to ten degrees. Fortunately for the lad, Shadow, his Labrador retriever, journeyed with him.

Shadow helped keep Greg alive by huddling against him and licking his face as the boy grew weary and discouraged and plopped down. When rescuers found the youngster nine hours later, the dog was lying across his lap, placing his body's warmth on his friend.

"It was, like, scary," the sixth-grader told an interviewer later that evening.[4] Apparently, the two had ventured farther into the woods than planned. "Shadow laid down next to me and he kept his head on my legs and he'd lick me in the face," Greg announced. "He kept me warm."

Shadow. Nice name for a dog who follows you everywhere.

Spirit. Nice name for a deity who walks alongside us everywhere, through all danger. Can't say I recall being licked in the face by the Spirit, but times without number, Man's *Best* Friend has saved me.

---

4. "He had his Shadow to keep him warm // Dog keeps boy alive during ordeal in woods," *Tampa Bay Tribune*, July 6, 2006.

No Bull

"Jump between them, Randall! Run! Jump between them!"

My Mississippi Delta father-in-law purchased a massive, muscular, aggressive 2,000-pound Black Angus bull, which he intended to use in siring Black Angus calves. The behemoth must service the right cows—Black Angus heifers or other Angus cows—in order to produce prize-winning, "top-dollar" show calves and money-makers. But the angry, cooped-up bull with business in his eye is loose from his pen and charging toward an unsuspecting, crossbred heifer.

"Jump between them, Randall! Run! Jump between them! Quick! Don't let him have his way with that heifer!"

"Sir?"

"Don't let him do it! Jump between them! Hurry!"

"But . . ."

"Never mind. Too late."

"I'm sorry, but I—"

"Done now. Man, I hate that! Don't take 'em long. Wish you coulda jumped between 'em."

"I'm sorry, but I . . ."

"That's all right. Don't worry 'bout it. Doggone it! C'mon, nothing we can do 'bout it now. Let's get him back in the pen."

"Mr. Donahoe, I'm really sorry. I'm honored to be your son-in-law. You're a big man, a great man, and I love and respect you. Would do anything in the world for you. But there's one thing I won't do: I won't bear you a bouncing baby calf."

Schoolboy Memories of Schoolgirl Moments

One high school Friday night, Dwight Stockton, Jimmy Brumfield, and I receive some welcome communication from Amy Felder. "Dixie Stokes and Diane Crawford are spending the night at my house, and you guys are welcome to come by later tonight if you want to."

After taking a bath in English Leather cologne, I feel up to the challenge. We guys pile headlong into Dwight's Volkswagen Beetle and make our way to Amy's, where her parents have retired to their chambers for the evening, leaving the girls the living room for entertaining. We arrive smelling like a cologne factory, all wearing English Leather, the lady-killing fragrance of the day, and, of course, our favorite shirts. Mine is a madras plaid from Denman Alford's, where I paid way too much at "The In-Place to Shop."

Dwight, a handsome starter on our high school basketball team, had dated Amy for several months but recently broken up with her. He is now dating Dixie. Diane has a crush on Jimmy. That leaves me with Amy—not a bad place to be since she has something to prove versus Dixie.

Under lamplight only, listening to soft music, we laugh and smooch the night away. I cannot be certain Amy remembers the night. Considering my dripping-wet drenching in English Leather, she likely was intoxicated on the fumes.

***

Nora Hickman is cute. She is cheering on the sidelines of a football game when quarterback Gary Boyd calls a pass-play in the huddle, where I will sprint down the right sideline in front of the cheerleaders. Adrenaline-dizzy at the prospect of impressing Nora, perhaps with a touchdown right in front of her, I break huddle, speed out of the backfield, cut right, and streak down the right sideline. Running alone, I am wide open. But Gary, receiving pressure, has to throw the ball sooner than I expect. As I turn to look for the ball, it explodes in my helmet earhole, sending me sprawling at Nora's feet.

***

Our high school basketball team annually travels to North Pike High School to play our county rivals. I am a sophomore, my first year on the squad. Senior stars and pranksters Robbie DeCoux and Bubba Walker steal my athletic supporter from my travel bag and hide it. As Coach Bennie Kimble, whom I later learn is in on the prank, stands at the door hollering for us to hit the floor with desire, I only want to hit the floor fully clothed. I cannot find my necessary equipment, also known as "jock strap," anywhere!

As the buzzer ends the game that night, Cheerleader Nora heads straight toward me on the court. My heart beats out of control as I feel certain she wants to walk me off the court. As she reaches me, she shouts, "Did you know you're so skinny, when you shoot your jump-shot we can count your ribs?"

Believe me. It could have been much worse!

Unforgettable Allison Dickson

"Fooled ya, didn't I?" Allison Dickson smiles from her motorized wheelchair. Diagnosed with Werdnig-Hoffmann, a rare form of muscular dystrophy, at the age of fifteen months, Allison was given one year to live.

Despite that prediction, Allison graduated *summa cum laude* from college with a double major in English and psychology, received the Outstanding English Student of the Year Award, the Outstanding Psychology Student of the Year Award, and the Outstanding Student Leader Award on her campus. She also received her Phi Beta Kappa Key.

Werdnig-Hoffmann causes paralysis and severe dehydration, which necessitate breathing treatments three times daily and sometimes hospitalization. Her determination to be a lawyer in order to help others, however, could never be denied.

The joy of knowing Allison fell upon me when she enrolled in a law school class in Oral Advocacy that I team-taught. A central focus of the class recognized and promoted the power of stories in moving individuals, audiences, judges, and juries toward desired decisions.

One of our class assignments afforded students the opportunity to present a closing argument to the class or, if one desired, a homily. Allison chose the homily. Her moving autobiographical message was titled "It's Not What We Get, It's What We Give." My recollections follow, enhanced by the publication of her address in *Docket Call*

(Winter 2006), the magazine of the Baylor Law School, from which these quotes appear.

"We are God's hands on Earth, created both to receive help and to give it," Allison began, exuding love. "By giving of ourselves to others, we follow God's example and spread His love." Then she shared a story.

George was a man whom you might say was far from handsome. Along with being short, he had a hunchback. One day he visited a friend with a beautiful daughter named Sarah. George immediately fell hopelessly in love with her, but she was repulsed by his unusual appearance.

George attempted to talk to Sarah many times, but she always gave him the cold shoulder. When the time came for George to leave, he gathered his courage, pulled Sarah aside, and took one last opportunity to speak with her. Again, she could barely look at him. And then, shyly, he asked her, "Sarah, do you believe marriages are made in heaven?" Still looking at the floor, she answered, "Yes. And do you?" "Yes, I do," he replied. "You see, in heaven, when each boy is born, the Lord shows him which girl he will marry. When I was born, the Lord pointed out my future bride, and she had a hunchback. Right then and there I called out, 'Oh, Lord, a hunchback woman would be a tragedy. Please, Lord, give me the hunchback and let her be beautiful.'"

Sarah looked into his eyes and her heart stirred. She slowly reached out, gave George her hand, and later became his devoted wife.

It's not what you get, it's what you give.

After finishing first in her law school class and first in our hearts, today Allison is a successful attorney in Texas, *giving* herself to help others, *giving* God's love to all, and *giving* the world an unforgettable person.

HYPOCRISY

Giving Christ a Black Eye

"Hey kid, are you a k***?"

"I don't know." The little boy had never heard the word before.

"Are you a Christ-killer?"

"I don't know."

"Where do you live?" the gang demanded.

The young boy told them.

"So you *are* a k***! You are a Christ-killer! Well, you're in Christian territory, and we are Christians. We're going to teach you to stay where you belong."

Years later, the boy, Mike Gold, revealed in his book *A Jew Without Knowing It* that his mother had warned him not to wander beyond four streets. Mike had wandered too far.

In his book *Why Am I Afraid to Love?*, John Powell retells the lad's story. He relates how the child was beaten, bloodied, and taunted as the gang sent him home, shouting, "We are Christians, and you killed Christ! Stay where you belong!"

When Mike's mother saw her young son, she became hysterical. "Who did this to you?"

"I don't know," the frightened boy answered.

As his mother held and rocked her young son to soothe him, he whispered to her, "Mama, who is Christ?"

The most prominent philosopher of American Communism in the 1920s was a Jewish man named Mike Gold—yes, this *same* Mike

Gold. Powell shares that Gold died in 1967, taking his last meals in a Catholic charity run by Dorothy Day in New York City.

Day said of Gold, "Mike Gold eats every day at the table of Christ, but he will probably never accept him because of the day he first heard his name."

Looking Glass

Traveling to and from work each day, I pass a deep curiosity: a building. Something is manufactured on the site, yet the front of the facility resembles an ultra-modern office complex with stunning mirrored glass presenting an elegant face. Only by viewing the sides of the large complex can one discern that this is, in fact, a factory and not a suite of professional offices.

Regrettably, however, the majestic appearance of the edifice is marred. In the place of several large panels of front mirrored glass stand three unsightly sheets of plywood. Neglect and ill repair over the years have sadly resulted in a snaggle-tooth smile to this otherwise striking site.

Recently, I noticed their empty parking lot on successive days. The plant had closed its doors. Operations ceased. Guess what I learned this failed business once produced? Enhanced glass! That's the company name. Or was. Enhanced Glass. No wonder their façade captured the eye!

But alas, years passed. In time the company no longer used its own product, even though it continued to seek to sell to others. First stage: They stopped modeling their own product. Second stage: Others noticed. Third stage: Business suffered. Fourth stage: Doors closed. Fifth stage: Town talk. Sixth stage: Embarrassment. Shame. Grief.

The other day while I drove by the failed enterprise, shaking my head at the sad situation, a sinking feeling came over me as Enhanced Glass turned into a Looking Glass.

"And you? What about you, Preacher O'Brien? Do *you* still use the product you sell?"

Stealing Credit

The football team at Ouachita Baptist University in Arkansas had an open date on its schedule. Head Coach Buddy Bob Benson decided to let the players go home for the weekend. Quarterback Scott Street only had one class on Friday afternoon. By missing that class, he could leave campus at noon and arrive home much earlier. The temptation was too hard to resist.

Scott approached one of his best friends, also enrolled in the course. "If I decide to leave early, would you turn in my homework assignment for me?"

"Sure. No sweat. Be happy to turn it in for you."

So Scott took off. After a restful weekend, Scott returned to school and class on Monday. Toward the end of his afternoon class the professor, uncharacteristically, returned homework assignments. Everyone received a paper except Scott. When his friend's name, who sat next to him, was called, Scott noticed something strange. His friend's handwriting looked exactly like his. Couldn't be. Could it?

Nervous behavior. No eye contact. "Hey, what's going on? Lemme see that paper! What did you do?"

You guessed it. Scott's close friend had erased Scott's name and substituted his own name on the assignment. He stole the credit due his friend!

"I can't believe this!" Scott shouted. "Why? Why did you do this?"

Years later, I heard Scott relate the story to a Christian audience. He refused to name his friend. But he did tell on someone else: "I've thought about that disillusionment a lot. Only time something like that ever happened to me. But you know what? I do the same thing all the time. I erase God's name from his work and write my own name on it. All the time. Success, health, job, wife. I steal his credit every chance I get. I am guilty. *Guilty!*"

Can anybody else relate? Have you focused on the guilt of others while stealing credit from God? *Ouch!* Methinks I know the poor soul who sets the curve in that class.

The Gold-embossed Funeral Invitation

"Look at this. Ever see anything like this?"

"What is it?" Kay asks, walking towards me where I stand at the kitchen counter opening the day's mail.

"Well, I don't know. Never seen anything like it."

There we pause, staring at the solid black envelope addressed in gold calligraphic script. Containing a striking ebony funeral invitation, the embossed gold letters reads, "The honor of your presence is requested for the funeral, Saturday, February 4, 2017, 10:00 a.m. U.S. Knoxville National Cemetery, Knoxville, Tennessee."

"Who is it from?" Kay asks.

"I don't know. Doesn't say."

"That's strange."

"Sure is."

"Who died?"

"Don't know. Doesn't say that either."

"Well, what are you going to do?"

"Beats me."

"Someone must want you there."

"Yeah, I reckon, unless it's a mistake."

"But it's got your name on the envelope."

"Sure does. Strange."

Saturday morning comes. After a bowl of oatmeal and a cup of coffee, I move to the bedroom closet and reach for my dark suit, white shirt, and navy blue tie.

"Where are you going?"

"Reckon I'll drive over to that funeral in Knoxville."

"Seriously?"

"Sure. Guess I feel I should. Besides, I admit I'm pretty curious. You stay here and relax. I got this."

Completing my forty-minute drive from our nearby town to the Knoxville cemetery, I motor slowly around the burial grounds until I see a line of parked cars near a tented fresh grave site. Parking at the end of the line, I exit my automobile and amble to the edge of the gathering.

Coats are the fashion of the morning. *I'm glad I listened to Kay and wore mine*, I think, as the early morning February air chills us. I recognize no one. The ritual begins. The minister in the black suit reads from the Bible, "Thou shalt love thy neighbor as thyself." Then he tears the page out of the Good Book, drops it into the fresh grave, and remarks somberly, "We do not live by these words anymore. Let us give them a decent burial."

The Reverend next reads from the Sermon on the Mount, "Do unto others as you would have them do unto you." Gently separating the page from the Holy Book, releasing it to float to the bottom of the pit, he intones, "We pay our respects to the Golden Rule, which no longer lives in our midst."

Visiting other noble verses from the Bible, the mysterious Man-o'-the-Cloth slowly dislodges each page, sending one after another to its grave.

"Love your enemies." "Pray for those who persecute you." "Be kind to one another." "Make love your aim." "Do justice, love kindness, walk humbly with your God."

One by one each descends into the pit.

"Ashes to ashes, dust to dust," announces the Reverend. "These words, now deceased, return to their Author."

"Let us pray," he whispers softly. "O Lord, forgive us this day our daily dead. For we have crucified your words as we crucified you. Amen."

Quietly, slowly, I turn, walk subdued to my car, and motor home. In silence.

The Least Understood of All God's Commandments

Growing up in Mississippi, we all had guns, knives, bows and arrows. The menfolk would find us in the crib, break through the womenfolk, and growl, "Here boy, here's your 12-gauge shotgun!" Short years later, we boys played games of chicken to prove our manhood, to accelerate our rite of passage from boy to man.

One game of chicken called for us to find an open field, encircle it, put two contestants in the large circle fifty yards or so apart, and then see who would "chicken" first as we shot arrows at each other. Now, there were rules. The arrows had to be shot high in the air and arched in on the target rather than shot straight at one's opponent. As the arrows were "walked in" closer and closer, whoever moved first "chickened" and must leave the circle. Another took his place and so on, until only a winner remained, a real MAN!

Another game of chicken involved knives. We all had them. Pocket knives, hunting knives, or, if nothing else, snitched kitchen knives. We would form a circle, two of us standing barefooted in the middle, two or three steps apart facing each other. With legs spread wide, we took turns throwing our knife into the ground between our opponent's feet. Then our feet would move closer together as the danger was repeated. Again and again the knives flew until our feet were only inches apart. Who would "chicken"?

One day is etched in my memory. Butch and Rocky Johnson, tough brothers tenth months apart in age, found themselves in the circle battling for manhood and sibling superiority. Butch, the older one, was an inch shorter; Rocky, the younger, weighed ten pounds more. The rivalry was fierce.

In the showdown's first move, Butch cockily deferred. Rocky threw. The blade pierced the ground between Butch's feet. Butch fired back, his sharp missile tearing the ground beneath Rocky. Legs drew closer together. Rocky hurled his dagger with precision. Butch slung his cutting edge with intimidating speed. We were all nervous around the circle. The showdown raged. Each of the brothers' feet now stood a hand's width apart. Neither brother blinked. Rocky cast his knife skillfully in the narrow opening. Butch speedily responded, sending his steel into the arch of his brother's bare foot. Blood shot upward. Rocky screamed, "God d*$#!"

We froze. The blood froze. Rocky took the name of the Lord our God in vain! Nobody moved. Slowly, one by one, we backed away from Rocky. It was over. Rocky was going to hell.

Years later, I learned Rocky might not be in Hell. *Had* Rocky violated the mysterious command, which remains the least understood of all God's commandments? What does the ancient mandate actually mean?

"Name" refers to character. The Hebrew word, which translates "vain," means "falsely, or a lie." To call upon God's name falsely, or to take God's name falsely upon oneself, is to commit the sin of blasphemy, i.e., to blaspheme God's character, while claiming to do otherwise. To my knowledge, Rocky never claimed to represent God in those days.

Maybe I should be more troubled by my own conduct than Rocky's.

Maybe.

Maybe I'm too chicken.

FORGIVENESS

Did Moses Ever Throw a Chair?

I know Moses led the children of Israel out of bondage in Egypt to the edge of the Promised Land. I know he raised his rod and parted the sea. I know the Great Man brought the Ten Commandments down from the mountain. I know he even killed a man down in Egypt-land. But did he ever throw a chair?

I know Jacob swindled his brother out of his birthright. Abraham lied about his wife. David and Bathsheba were married to others, when they—shall we say—got to know each other. Peter denied Christ three times. Paul persecuted Christians. But did any of them ever throw a chair?

I know American presidents Thomas Jefferson, James Buchanan, Grover Cleveland, Warren Harding, Franklin Roosevelt, Dwight Eisenhower, Lyndon Johnson, John Kennedy, Bill Clinton, and Donald Trump, among others, are said to have engaged in sexual affairs. But did any of these ever throw a chair?

When I was in college, a young man on our campus ardently led a Christian life. He participated in a Bible study group taught by a seminarian, led another one, and, when invited, gave his Christian testimony in churches. He was a leader in the Fellowship of Christian Athletes.

One night, as he and his team played poorly in a well-attended intramural basketball game on campus, our young Christian exemplar began to lose his composure. The player guarding our Christian disciple embarrassed him routinely on both ends of the court with superior play, defensively and offensively. Tempers flared. Elbows struck. Pushing and shoving drew penalties.

Timeout was called to calm players, especially you-know-who. Our young devout follower of Jesus refused even to go to the sidelines. With his cool completely lost, he angrily took a seat in a metal folding chair courtside opposite the players' benches. When he refused to come to the bench, the coach had little recourse but to insert a substitute player into the game. Referees called for play to resume. The ball was thrown in-bounds.

Instantly, our champion for Christ leaped up and threw his chair across the court. Then he, with the game stopped and all eyes fixed on him, strutted slowly across the court and flopped down on the end of the team bench.

Silence.

I will always remember that night. How could I forget it? I remember how that young man lost so much more than a basketball game. I'll always remember it for several reasons; I'll never forget it . . . because I'm that guy.

Shame. Guilt. Humiliation. I feel so ashamed. I live with the pain of memories. Haunting guilt. Embarrassment!

Have you ever "blown it"? Moses did. Jacob did. Abraham did. David and Bathsheba did. Peter did. Paul did. And boy, I have!

We've all "blown it," haven't we? I hope we won't miss the life-changing teaching of the Good Book:

Our God doesn't give up on people.

Amen?

Forgiveness for Foolin' Around

The account of the woman caught in the act of adultery ranks as one of the most memorable stories in the New Testament (John 8). Surprisingly, the oldest manuscripts of the Gospel contain no mention of the narrative. For reasons unknown to us, the original writer decided against its inclusion. As the story persisted in oral form, however, John, or a later scribe, chose to add it to the document called the Gospel According to John.

Why? Why would the story persist in oral tradition, and why would John or a later scribe add the account to the Fourth Gospel? Ideas may vary, but surely the wisdom, warmth, and forgiveness of Jesus encouraged others that their sins, too, meet the same gracious forgiveness from Christ. So the good news could not be contained, spreading widely through the telling of the beloved story:

"Teacher, this woman has been caught in adultery, in the very act. The law of Moses says to stone the woman; what do you say?"

"He who is without sin among you, let him be the first to throw a stone at her."

. . . "Woman, where are your accusers? Did no one condemn you?"

"No one, Lord."

"Neither do I condemn you. Go and sin no more."

This story serves several priceless purposes, including these two: encouragement that our sins might also be forgiven and encouragement to follow Jesus' example of forgiveness.

My maternal grandmother incarnated "priceless purpose #2." Mamaw had eleven children, each of whom had children of their own. Most of the children and grandchildren lived "in the country." Our family lived "in town." During the summer months, I spent a lot of time "out in the country" playing with my cousins. When I was ten, one of my male cousins told me the story.

"Freddie Jean and Bobby Dale [names changed] got caught doing it," he said.

"Our cousins?" I asked.

"You know any other Freddie Jeans and Bobby Dales?"

"No. But they're cousins."

"Don't matter none. They were doing it."

"The real grown-up thing?"

"Yep. The real grown-up thing."

"How do you know?"

"Bobby Dale told me."

"Where were they?"

"Mamaw's house."

"Are they crazy?"

"Yep. Mamaw caught 'em, too."

"You're kiddin'! How d'ya know?"

"Bobby Dale told me."

"What'd she do?"

"She told 'em to get dressed. Told 'em how disappointed she was. Said she'd forgive 'em and never say a word about it to anyone if they promised never to do it again."

"What did Freddie Jean and Bobby Dale do?"

"They put their clothes on and promised never to do it again."

Over the next seven years until my Mamaw passed away, I watched her around my cousins, Freddie Jean and Bobby Dale. Sometimes the gatherings were large, like family reunions; sometimes the get-togethers were small, involving only three or four families. Mamaw seemed to favor Freddie Jean and Bobby Dale as much as she did any of us. It was like she had no memory of things at all. She just loved her grandchildren beautifully. All secrets were safely stored away, or forgotten, in her love.

In my first book of stories published fifteen years ago, this memory was not included. However, I've never been able to forget Mamaw's loving forgiveness toward my cousins. Her loving grace and forgiveness encourage me daily to live and love and forgive like Mamaw. So, like John, I'm adding a story that just won't go away.

Now I Know How John the Baptist Felt

The ringing telephone taunted me until I finally turned and picked up the receiver. "This is Randall O'Brien."

"Dr. O'Brien, this is Harold Henry. I'm wondering if there might be a time I could meet with you this week. It's very important."

"Sure, Harold. I'd be happy to visit with you. How about Friday? 3:00 p.m.? I have that time open. How does that sound?"

"Friday at 3 would be fine, Dr. O'Brien. Thank you very much. I'll see you then. This is very important."

My curiosity grew as Friday approached, then arrived. "Hello, Harold," I greeted my octogenarian guest. Nice to meet you. C'mon in. Please have a seat. Can I get you a cold drink?"

"No, I'm fine, thank you. Thank you very much for seeing me, Dr. O'Brien. This matter has really been bothering me. I just had to come talk to you."

"Well, I'm glad you did, Harold. Please. Tell me. How can I help?"

"Dr. O'Brien, I did a terrible thing. I've never done anything like this before or since. But I just had to come tell you what I did."

"Sure. I'm glad you came, Harold. Why don't you tell me about it?"

"Dr. O'Brien, I cheated on a test at Baylor in 1949. It wasn't the final exam, but I cheated just the same. My conscience is killing me!"

"Harold, how old are you?"

"I'm eighty-one."

"You're eighty-one. This is 2007. You cheated on an exam in 1949, nearly sixty years ago, and your conscience is killing you?"

"It sure is. I've never confessed my sin, Dr. O'Brien. Never told anyone about it until now."

"My goodness."

"You see, I've been praying for revival to come to my church. Yet here I sit with this unconfessed sin in my life. God has really been speaking to me about my own sin. I felt I had to come to you as the Executive Vice President and Provost of Baylor and turn myself in to you."

"Harold, are you familiar with that verse in the Bible which declares, 'If we say we have no sin we deceive ourselves and the truth is not in us; but if we confess our sin, he is faithful and just to forgive us our sin and to cleanse us from all unrighteousness'?"

"I sure am, Dr. O'Brien. That's 1 John, chapter 1, verses 8 and 9."

"Well, it seems to me that Scripture pretty much settles it for us."

"But what about Baylor?"

"Harold, as Executive Vice President and Provost of Baylor University, by the power and authority vested in me by the President and the Board of Regents, I do hereby pardon you for your wrongdoing in 1949. God has forgiven you; Baylor has pardoned you. Go now, and with the rest of us sinners, celebrate God's marvelous grace."

"Whew!" My visitor's chest relaxed as he exhaled his guilt and then inhaled God's grace. Sighing joyfully, smiling happily, he whispered, "Thank you, thank you, thank you! May we pray?"

As we bowed our heads, Harold prayed like an angel. A paradox pierced my peace. One such as I receiving the confession of one such as he? Remember the baptism of Jesus by John the Baptist? Now I know how John felt.

I Confessed My Sin to Billy Graham

"Would you like to meet Daddy?" Ruth Graham asked Kay and me one evening after dinner in our home in March 2013.

Like most people on Planet Earth it seemed, I practically idolized Billy Graham. The Reverend had served as "Pastor to the President" to every United States president from Dwight Eisenhower forward: Eisenhower, Kennedy, Johnson, Nixon, Ford, Carter, Reagan, Bush, Clinton, G. W. Bush, and Obama. Since Mr. Graham preached his first crusade in Los Angeles in 1949, he went on to preach 417 crusades to more than 214 million people in 195 cities and territories, more than any other person in history. Between 1955 and 2013, he appeared 56 times in the Gallup Poll's "10 Most Admired Men in the World."

"Would I like to meet Billy Graham? Are you serious?"

"Of course, I'm serious. We could drive over to our home on Black Mountain in North Carolina and spend some time with Daddy. Would you like that?"

And that's how I ended up hearing Billy Graham's daughter introduce us.

"Daddy, this is Kay and Randall O'Brien I was telling you about. Randall is President of Carson-Newman University. These are my dear friends."

"Hello, Dr. Graham. Kay and I are honored to meet you."

"It's good to meet you, Dr. and Mrs. O'Brien. I'm sorry you had to drive all the way over here. I wish I could have come over to your place, maybe given a little talk or something."

"Oh, no sir, the honor of being here is all ours."

"Dr. Graham," Kay added, "we know you are proud of Ruth. She's one of our best friends, and such a wonderful ambassador for Christ, like her daddy. Thank you for sharing her with us."

"Ruth is named for her mother, you know. Yes, I am very proud of her."

"Dr. Graham, we have something we'd like to present to you," I shared. "Carson-Newman University has named you 'Evangelist of the 20th Century.' We would like to present this engraved crystal award to you for your inspirational faithfulness to Jesus Christ and preaching of His Gospel."

"Oh, my. While I do not deserve this award, I accept it in the name of the One whom I have sought to serve all my life. It is especially meaningful to receive this from a school well known for shaping hearts and minds of next-generation students for Jesus Christ."

"We believe you *do* deserve it and are blessed to be here to present the award to you."

"Thank you. May I say a prayer for you and your school?"

Following the saint's prayer, I announced I had a surprise confession to make. "Reverend Graham, I need to confess something to you."

"You do?"

"Yes sir. I do. As a young college student, I checked out of our school library a biography of Billy Graham written by John Pollock. I read it, loved it—and kept it. I always meant to mail the book back, but never did. I married, finished seminary, and began ministry. Finally, the guilt was just too great. I mailed the book back to the school's library, along with a check for the price of a new book. The college librarian was gracious, writing me a nice note thanking me for returning the volume. I surely did feel better. I feel better now, too, telling you about it."

The great man smiled. "Your sins are forgiven. Go and sin no more."

Well, I'll Be Doggone, but He Wasn't

"I can get you a registered Old English sheepdog puppy if you want one," fellow grad student Sam Hawkins announced to me one day on campus.

"Really? Where?"

"I know someone who has a litter; sellin' 'em for $300."

"I dunno. That's a lot o' money for a starvin', married grad student."

"Not for a registered Old English sheepdog. Think I might get one."

"I dunno what Kay might say about it in my house."

"Well, lemme know if you want one, but you'd probably better decide pretty soon, or they'll all be gone."

***

"Honey, I got a surprise for you!"

"Oh, you do? What kind of surprise?"

"One you're gonna love!"

"Really?"

"Yep! Come in; sit down on the couch, and close your eyes."

"What makes me suspicious about this?"

"Okay, you can open 'em now."

"O my gosh! Honey, what is this? What have you done?"

"Isn't he precious? I bought him from a guy Sam Hawkins knows. It's a present for you. Isn't he gorgeous?"

"Yes, he's cute as can be; but you bought him for *me*, did ya? I think I know your tricks. You didn't buy him for me. You bought him for *you*!"

"Okay, how 'bout for *us*?"

"Honey, what are we gonna do with a dog? He's cute as can be, but do you know how big these dogs get?"

"Yes, I do. Don't you just love him? Look! He *likes* you, honey! He can be our first son!"

"*Randall O'Brien*!"

RACE

A Black Pastor, A White Deacon, and a New Day

Reverend Andrew W. Gilmore, African American pastor of Greater Tulane Missionary Baptist Church and Christian Love Missionary Baptist Church in New Orleans in the 1970s, was the proud father of a beautiful daughter. A Caucasian Methodist minister in town was the proud father of a handsome son. The two ministers preached a Christian gospel of brotherly love, equality, and racial reconciliation. The children took their fathers' sermons to heart.

When the ministers' children began dating each other, the clergymen found their faith tested. How equal are White and Black people? Is interracial dating acceptable? And if so, is it advisable? Racial tension gripped the city in those years. Danger lurked, as it did in much of the South in the 1960s and '70s.

One Saturday as the two young lovers enjoyed a picnic on the shore of Lake Pontchartrain in the city, they found themselves surrounded by a group of ne'er-do-wells, White males. The brigands beat the young man severely, breaking both of his arms, rendering him helpless to defend his girlfriend. They broke Coke bottles and repeatedly sliced her angelic face.

Word spread fast throughout the city. African Americans, raging on the verge of rioting, gathered at night on the campus of the

University of New Orleans. Emerging in the darkness of the explosive evening appeared Reverend Gilmore. Striding to the stage, he began,

> Many of you know our daughter. She is in intensive care tonight. Extensive plastic surgery is required to repair her face. I am speaking calmly, but inside I am boiling. Anger at wrong is right. We are right to be here tonight. Both of her boyfriend's arms are broken, set in casts. It will take time for our loved ones to heal. But they will not get well any sooner if we hurt other people. Dr. King says we must return love for hate. We must love our enemies and pray for them. Our anger must not lead us to hate, but to change our world. Non-violent change. Violence cannot defeat evil. Only love can do that. I thank you for coming out tonight. I want us to pray. Then I want us to go home and keep praying. We will resist hatred peacefully. Love will win. God will win. Evil will lose, unless it takes root in our hearts. Then evil will win. Let us pray. Let us love our enemies. Let us win their hearts, and usher in a new day.

Kay and I were the only White members of Rev. Gilmore's congregation in the 1970s. We loved Rev. and Mrs. Gilmore, and they loved us. When it came time for me to be ordained into the ministry, I wanted our pastor to preach my ordination sermon. Who else but a man like this?

Roundaway Baptist Church in Sunflower County, Mississippi, Kay's home church in the Mississippi Delta, was proud of our ministry in the ghettos of New Orleans. Church leadership beamed when we asked to be ordained in Kay's home church.

Until.

Until it was learned that I had invited the Reverend Andrew W. Gilmore, our New Orleans pastor, to preach my ordination sermon. The Reverend, Mrs. Gilmore, and two or three carloads of our African American sisters and brothers from our Louisiana church were planning on driving the five-hour distance to the Mississippi Delta to attend the worship service and dinner on the grounds to follow.

There was a problem.

Churches were not integrated in Mississippi in 1977, certainly not in the Mississippi Delta, where African Americans had long labored in cotton fields as slaves, Freedmen, sharecroppers, and tenant farmers but never as members of White churches. In Mississippi, most White congregations had never even allowed Black people to clean or cook in their segregated churches. A meeting of the Roundaway church membership was called.

According to my mother-in-law's testimony to Kay afterwards, many in the church thought the ordination service should be scheduled somewhere else. People became rather excited over the issue of carloads of African Americans arriving for the Roundaway Baptist Church worship service. Emotional back-and-forth erupted!

My father-in-law, a longtime deacon in the church, never said a word about it to us, but this is the story we received:

"It sort of got ugly," Kay's mother told her sometime after the meeting. "The church appeared to be moving in the direction of recommending that Randall be ordained somewhere else, like maybe his own home church in McComb." She didn't say a whole lot more but did add this word: "Until your daddy spoke! Your daddy, honey, can be a passionate, strong-willed man; but I don't know when I've seen him that passionate, even tearful, voice quivering, with such powerful words. But I'll tell you this. When he finished, they voted to have the ordination."

Bronze Star for Brenda

Civil rights heroes and heroines number in the hundreds, nay thousands, tens of thousands, from the 1960s alone. Many of our country's bravest soldiers earned their medals of valor on battlefields of strange names: lunch counters, bus stations, courthouses, public schools, jails. By rights, Purple Hearts should have rained upon crowded jail cells and bare backs in darkened forests where Satan's army tortured God's precious children of color. There, hooded hoodlums and Klansmen cops dispensed pain to prophets, wounds to warriors, evil to any who courageously worked for racial equality.

Jesus was an African American in the 1960s. Anti-Christ Christians and other hate-filled infidels killed him—again. And again and again and . . . again.

Wasn't that a crucifixion on the balcony of the Lorraine Hotel in Memphis in 1968? Didn't Chaney, Schwerner, and Goodman precede Dr. King on Golgotha in Philadelphia, Mississippi, in 1964? Wasn't Medgar Evers nailed at Calvary by a bullet to the back in Jackson in 1963? And what about the nearly anonymous Amite County farmer-messiah, Herbert Lee? What happened to him in September of '61?

All of these are heroes, fallen heroes, national heroes, and heroes of mine. There are thousands more. One, a young African American girl from McComb, Mississippi, stands out.

On Saturday, August 26, 1961, Mississippians Hollis Watkins and Curtis (Elmer) Hayes, both African American, sat in at Woolworth's

"Whites only" lunch counter in my hometown of McComb, thereby becoming the first people to take direct action against segregation in the state. For their revolutionary bravery, they were promptly arrested and jailed for thirty days and charged with breach of peace.

Four days later on Wednesday, August 30, 1961, Robert Talbert, Isaac Lewis, and fifteen-year-old Brenda Travis sat in at the segregated Greyhound bus station in McComb. They, too, were arrested immediately and incarcerated twenty-eight days in the county jail.

When Ike and Brenda were expelled from Burgland High, McComb's high school for African Americans, and then refused readmission, they were, in effect, handed lifetime sentences of punishing poverty. Southern Black people with high school educations could not, as a rule, expect to earn a fair, living wage. But to be denied the opportunity to earn even a high school diploma represented cruel and unusual punishment, a sentence of raw poverty for life.

On October 4, 1961, approximately 120 of Brenda's and Ike's classmates angrily protesting the expulsions and the oppressive culture of racial discrimination marched from Burgland High School through town, led by young Brenda, to the steps of City Hall singing, "We Shall Overcome." One by one the students ascended the steps of City Hall to kneel and pray. There they were beaten and kicked by cops and other fine Christian citizens, then arrested.

Brenda related years later, "I believe I was predestined to become an activist. I joined the NAACP and became involved in the movement to get people to vote. But they were afraid."

Jailed again, this time for their role in the student march, Brenda and the other students sang and prayed through the night. After several days, "They took me out of jail," Brenda related. "Said, 'We're taking you to Jackson to see your attorney.' After a long drive they pulled the car up to the gates of the Reform School in Oakley. My family, nobody knew where I was. My mother was never allowed to visit me the whole time. My family suffered."

Though sentenced to a year in Reformatory School, the young teenager was released before completing her full term under one condition established by the governor: she must leave the state within twenty-four hours of her release!

Following forty-five years of exile, Brenda returned to Mississippi on June 21, 2006, for the forty-fifth anniversary of the 1961 direct action against segregation in Mississippi. Determined, I got in my automobile, pulled out of my driveway, and drove ten hours from my home in Texas to find Brenda in McComb. I had something to say to her; I had something to give her.

Following two days of recognitions, speeches, awards ceremonies, a moving graduation exercise nearly a half-century too late for the expelled seniors of the Burgland High Class of '62, and a final stirring address to a full house by Brenda Travis, the right moment arrived for me to approach Brenda. My heart raced.

"Brenda," I began, "I'm Randall O'Brien. I'm a minister and the Executive Vice President and Provost of Baylor University. I grew up in McComb."

"Oh, I'm very glad to meet you."

"No, the honor is all mine. You are a hero of mine. I was twelve years old when you sat in at the bus station and marched on City Hall. You were fifteen. Those remain, for me, two of the greatest acts of bravery in my lifetime."

"How very kind of you. Thank you, Randall."

"Brenda, what happened to you was one of the darkest travesties of justice in American history. I am ashamed; I am embarrassed; I am angry. I am also changed by you, by your life, your courage, your cries for justice. As you know," I continued, "our lives always travel down paths of continuation or compensation in the area of racial injustice, one or the other. Your witness, and the courageous work of your sisters and brothers, has been a huge influence upon my life. I've tried to live my life to help compensate for all the wrong done to African Americans. How can I say, 'Thank you,' Brenda, for who you are and for who you've helped me to become?"

Brenda tried to speak but couldn't. Her eyes filled with tears. We hugged. Slipping my right hand into my pants pocket, I clutched the gift I had for her, pulled it out, and placed it in Brenda's hand.

Leaning back from our embrace while looking into my heroine's eyes, still holding her hand, I whispered, "A few years after your civil rights battles for our country, I fought for our country on a different battlefield—in Vietnam. Sometimes in an imperfect world a person might need to fight for his country. But no one—*no one*—should ever have to fight her country!"

Nodding humbly in silent agreement, brown eyes floating in tears, Brenda stood still. We both did, planted on holy ground. "For my service in Vietnam I was awarded the Bronze Star," I said. "For *your* gallantry, Brenda, you were awarded Reform School and cruel exile from your home state and family. You were *so many times more heroic* than I ever was! I want you to have my Bronze Star, Brenda, for your heroism. You already have my admiration and my heart."

Weeping, plunging us into tearful embrace again, Brenda whispered to me through her sobs, "I don't know what to say."

"You don't have to say anything. I thought about saving my medals for my children," I confessed, "maybe giving my Bronze Star to my son, so my children would have something to remember me by. Then I thought, no, this is how I want to be remembered: Brenda Travis gave her youth for civil rights for all Americans; Daddy gave his Bronze Star to Brenda Travis."

Love Wins

The year was 1979. Johnny Lee Clary, Grand Dragon of the Ku Klux Klan, sat impatiently in a local radio studio awaiting the arrival of his debate opponent. The Reverend Wade Watts of McAlester, Oklahoma, head of the Oklahoma NAACP, served as pastor of a local church, which Clary, unsuccessfully, had tried to burn to the ground. They would soon meet face to face.

Reverend Watts arrived, saw the Klansman sitting defiantly in his white robe, walked over to him, extended his hand, smiled, and said, "I love you." Caught completely off guard, the Grand Dragon held out his hand and embraced the minister's hand of forgiveness.

Within ten years, Johnny Lee Clary rose to the rank of Imperial Wizard in the Klan. He was unable, however, to shake the gracious welcome, smile, and loving words of his archenemy, Reverend Watts. One fine day in 1989, Clary convened the Grand Council of the Klan. When all were seated, he rose and dropped a bombshell. *"I quit!"*

Within two years, Johnny Lee had surrendered his life to Christian ministry. After having tried futilely to run from the haunting witness of Reverend Watts, Clary phoned the African American minister.

"Reverend Watts, this is Johnny Lee Clary. You might not remember me."

"Oh, I remember you, son!"

"Reverend Watts, I quit the Klan."

"You did *what*?"

"I quit the Klan. I want to be a minister like you."

"You want to *what*?"

"I want to be a minister like you, loving everybody, Reverend Watts."

"Help me, Jesus! O Lord! Help me, Jesus!"

"Reverend, I've never been able to shake your words to me that day in the studio. I've run from them for ten years, day and night, and I'm through running. I'm tired. I surrender. I want to be a minister like you."

"Oh, son, will you come preach in my church?"

And so the Christian ministry of Johnny Lee Clary began.

The two unlikely brothers began traveling together throughout the South, preaching the gospel of love and racial reconciliation. They even protested together at KKK rallies. Clary formed a ministry called Operation Colorblind, Inc, to oppose racism. The two men continued to travel and preach together until Reverend Watts went home to be with his Lord.

Following Reverend Watts's death and until her own, Mrs. Watts shared with any who cared to listen, "Johnny Lee is like family to us. He never tires of telling us how much he loves us."

Pilgrim in a Racist Land

The story did not begin with me. And long after I am gone, the story will journey on into the ages. But the caravan did come by here. And I climbed aboard.

> Ohhh, dat Gospel train's a comin'
> I hear dat whistle blowin'
> Yassuh, dat Gospel train's a comin'
> Gonna ride it t'glory.

The gospel was the hope of African Americans in the segregated South when I was growing up in the 1950s and 1960s in Mississippi. African Americans looked forward to the day when that "Gospel train" would spring their sweet escape from a racist "hell on earth" and land them in the celestial bliss of a peaceful, just, eternal heaven. Some of us White people dreamed too.

I reckon all who climb aboard God's Freedom Train understand that the train departs from Egypt always and journeys long through the wilderness before arriving in the Promised Land. Six years after my birth in 1949, the United States Supreme Court handed down a historic decision in the *Brown v. Board of Education* case on Monday, May 17, 1954, ruling that segregation in public schools was unconstitutional. In response to the Supreme Court's decision, Thomas P. Brady (Circuit Court judge of the 14th District of Mississippi) published a book titled *Black Monday* in which he wrote, "The Negro purposes to breed up his inferior intellect and whiten his skin and 'blow out the light' in the White man's brain and muddy his skin." He continued his racist tirade using the most dehumanizing terms.[5] In 1963, Judge Brady was awarded a seat on the bench of the Mississippi Supreme Court.

Within two months of the *Brown v. Board of Education* decision, the White Citizens' Council (which came to be known as "the white-collar Klan" or "the reading and writing Klan") was formed on July 11, 1954, in Indianola, Mississippi. Two years later, the Mississippi Legislature established the Mississippi State Sovereignty Commission to maintain segregation. How vividly I recall the Freedom Rides undertaken by Black and White activists in 1961, who dared to travel on Trailways and Greyhound buses from Washington D.C. to New Orleans for the sole purpose of testing federal integration laws in bus stations throughout the South. I was eleven years old when the Freedom Riders—or "Friction Riders" as they were called in the Jackson, Mississippi, press—were severely beaten in Jackson and in my hometown of McComb, Mississippi.

Four days after Elmer Hayer and Hollis Watkins undertook the first direction action for integration in Mississippi by Mississippians by sitting at the Woolworth's lunch counter in McComb, another sit-in took place at the bus station in McComb. Two African American high school students, Brenda Travis and Isaac Lewis, were jailed for twenty-eight days. Soon thereafter, on October 4, Branda Travis and 120 African American high school students marched through the streets of McComb to the steps of City Hall, where they were beaten and arrested.

On September 30, 1962, riots broke out at the University of Mississippi after James Meredith became the first African American student to enroll. Two people were killed in the melee, and sixty U.S. marshals were injured. Less than one year later, on June 11, 1963, NAACP field secretary in Mississippi, Medgar Evers, was murdered in the driveway of his home in Jackson, shot in the back with a high-powered rifle fired by Byron de la Beckwith of the White Citizens' Council. The long, hot summer of 1964 lay just around the corner.

---

5. Brady, *Black Monday* (Winona, MS: Association of Citizens' Councils, 1955), 12.

The Mississippi Freedom Summer Project of 1964 was a well-coordinated civil rights campaign that brought to the state hundreds of college student volunteers and other civil rights activists from the North and California to work for racial equality. More than 200 volunteers came to Mississippi on June 20 to establish Freedom Voter Registration, Freedom Schools, and Freedom Medical and Legal Clinics. By June 21, three of the civil rights workers had disappeared. The bodies of James Chaney, Michael Schwerner, and Andrew Goodman were found August 4 outside Philadelphia, Mississippi.

Civil rights workers and Mississippi African Americans suffered horribly in the long, hot summer of 1964. Included in the litany of evils suffered by the innocent were 1,000 arrests, 80 beatings, 35 shootings, 35 church bombings, 30 home bombings, and 6 murders. The list is likely incomplete since it includes only crimes that were reported.

My hometown of McComb, located in Pike County in Southwest Mississippi, became known internationally in 1964 as "The Dynamite Capitol of the World" for its twenty acts of violence and sixteen bombings of churches and homes in defiance of civil rights advances. Is it any wonder Martin Luther King Jr. described to United States Attorney General Robert Kennedy the evil in McComb as a "Reign of Terror"?

Shame covered the city like smog. Our churches fell silent; our preachers developed laryngitis. The body of Christ looked nothing at all like Jesus. No tables of racism were overturned in the temple. No ministerial anger cried out against bigotry, hatred, or murder. Along with the Finance Committee, Fellowship Committee, and Youth Committee, my home church formed a "N—— Committee," composed of the biggest and meanest men in the church, who met each Sunday on the steps of the church with one job and only one job: while the pastor stood in the pulpit preaching about a God who loved everyone, a certain race of people must *never, ever* get through that door. Where had all the prophets gone?

In the early 1960s, fewer than 2 percent of Mississippi's African American population were registered to vote. Some counties did not have a single registered African American voter. Yet White supremacy and segregation, twin Southern traditions proudly inherited by each new generation through paternal bloodlines and ingested through mother's milk, were being threatened.

The moment a Southerner surrenders his life to Christ for a lifetime of Christian ministry, a crisis strikes. In the area of race relations, shall he follow a course of continuation or compensation? Shall he follow Christ or culture? Will there be a transfer of allegiance? Whom shall one now seek to please, earthly father or heavenly Father? Shall the minister follow society or Scripture? Which will it be: family or faith? The choice is hard. Religion would be much easier if ethics were not involved.

Kay and I concluded that there was no choice after all. Either Christ was Lord or he wasn't. Robert Frost's poem, "The Road Not Taken," expresses our own dilemma and decision:

> Two roads diverged in a yellow wood,
> and sorry I could not travel both
> and be one traveler, long I stood
> and looked down one as far as I could
> to where it bent in the undergrowth;
>
> Then took the other, as just as fair,
> and having perhaps the better claim,
> because it was grassy and wanted wear; . . .
>
> Yet knowing how way leads on to way,
> I doubted if I should ever come back.
>
> I shall be telling this one day with a sigh
> somewhere ages and ages hence:
> two roads diverged in a wood, and I—
> I took the one less traveled by,
> and that has made all the difference.

"The road taken" led us to minister in poor areas of New Orleans in the 1970s while I was in seminary. Soon we had joined an African American church in the inner city as its only two White members.

In time Kay was asked to serve as Sunday school superintendent and I was invited to serve as associate pastor. Our families tried hard to understand our calling to minister in this setting, and I believe they were successful in doing so. Their love and support blessed us.

When my ordination was scheduled in Kay's home church in the Mississippi Delta, the church fellowship and our families seemed pleased. When we revealed, however, that we wanted our pastor, the Reverend Andrew W. Gilmore of Christian Love Missionary Baptist Church in New Orleans, to preach my ordination sermon, celebration turned into chaos. An African American preach in the pulpit of an all-White Mississippi Delta church? In the very town in which the White Citizens' Council was formed? And wouldn't other African Americans want to make the trip from New Orleans as well?

Although my ordination in Roundaway Baptist Church in Sunflower County, Mississippi, created no small crisis, we remain very proud of the way in which the deacons and the church membership responded to the collision of segregation and Scripture. When Kay's father, a deacon in the church, delivered a passionate appeal to the church on behalf of right, the church followed the leadership of the Holy Spirit beautifully. The ordination service provided a glimpse of God's True Church where all believers are one in Christ Jesus.

We could not have known what awaited us in our first pastorate on the Mississippi-Louisiana state line. Rather than reveal the name of the church, I prefer the pseudonym "Southern Baptist Church." Moreover, all names are fictitious except in cases where a person lines up on the side of right. I am proud to make known the identities of the faithful.

"Are you going to homecoming this weekend?" I asked Doug Taylor one Tuesday afternoon in October 1979 as we walked across the campus of the New Orleans Baptist Theological Seminary. Doug and I had graduated from Mississippi College, he in 1978 and I in 1975.

"I'd love to, but I don't have a car," he lamented.

"Hey, that's no problem," I said. "Kay and I are going, and you are more than welcome to ride with us."

"For real?" he asked.

"Absolutely!" I said. And so the drama began innocently enough.

Kay and I planned to drive from New Orleans to Clinton, Mississippi, Friday afternoon, attend homecoming festivities at the college Saturday, then travel Saturday night to the church field where I served as pastor. Sunday we would worship morning and evening, then return to New Orleans late Sunday night. We never even thought about the obvious. Then it hit me. "Hon," I said, "I never once thought about this, but Doug is Black and Southern Baptist Church is White. We've got a problem."

"I never thought about it either," she said. "What are we going to do?"

"Well, maybe this is what God wants, even though we didn't think about what we were doing," I mused. "Let's talk to Doug, explain the situation, pray about it for a couple of days, and see what we think we should do."

"Doug, I've got to explain something to you," I began. With that, I told him that a Black person had never, ever been in the church, not even to cook or clean, and that the church sat in the heart of Klan territory, but that the invitation was still on the table. We agreed to pray. Thursday evening, the three of us met in our home to finalize our plans according to God's guidance through prayer. One by one we reported that our sense was "all systems go!" We had not intentionally plotted to integrate Southern Baptist Church. Despite our naivete, or maybe because of it, we felt providentially chosen by God for this historic act. If it is possible for fear and peace to coexist, those two polar neighbors seemed to find a home in our hearts.

Sunday morning arrived. Doug, Kay, and I, along with Eric Holleyman, our associate pastor for music and youth, prayed together at the parsonage and then drove to the church. Word traveled fast. As soon as Sunday worship concluded, Sammy Wilson ran up to me and exploded, "Ed Earl wants to see you right now! He said to tell you to get your *^%#! over to his house the minute church is out!"

Ed Earl was a church member who attended church every leap year. I suspected he was a Klansman, but I had no way of knowing. In order to present the false impression that I was not frightened, I ate Sunday lunch first rather than rush right over. Eric insisted on going with me. When we arrived at Ed Earl's, Jimmie Lou met us at the door and ushered us into the room where Ed Earl sat waiting. Jimmie Lou excused herself, closing the door behind her. Ed Earl said nothing for the longest. Then he began.

"Got a little visit this mornin'," he said. "The boys came by, tearin' into my driveway in their pick-up trucks, slingin' gravel everywhere, blowin' their horns, slammin' on brakes, throwin' rocks, and hollerin'—'Ed Earl, git out here quick!' Well, I went outside and said, 'What're you boys up to?' They said, 'Git in the truck, Ed Earl!' I said, 'Where you boys goin'?' They said, 'Git in the truck, Ed Earl! We're goin' to git us a n—— 'n a preacher!'

"Then they told me it was you! I was so mad I could *%^#! But I told 'em, 'I'm gonna have to ask you boys to turn around and go back home.' 'What!' they said. 'You heard me, boys. Lemme handle this one; I owe that preacher one; he's taken up a lot o' time with my boy, huntin', playin' ball. But I tell you what I'm gonna do. If it ever happens again, you won't be pickin' me up. I'll be pickin' you up! Now go on home. I'll take care of this one."

Ed Earl paused as he spoke—eyes watering, face beet red—then he looked me square in the eye, voice quivering, and threatened, "If it ever happens again . . ."

Ed Earl never finished his sentence. He didn't have to. I understood. My life was being threatened. "Ed Earl," I managed, "what are you asking me to do? To stand in that pulpit and preach about a God who loves everybody but put a sign in front of the church saying, 'No Negroes Allowed'? I can't do that, Ed Earl. You've gotta decide what you've gotta do; I've gotta do what God tells me to do." Ed Earl stared daggers through me. I felt I was peering into the face of death.

"It better not happen again!" he warned.

"Does tonight count?" I asked. "Because I can't tell a man who wants to worship God that he can't come in the church. I'm not going to do that, Ed Earl."

That evening before Doug, Kay, Eric, and I went to church we prayed, placing ourselves and the witness of that day in God's hands. The evening crowd nearly filled the sanctuary, which was unusual. Standing before the congregation, I reminded the worshipers that we had the right to choose the color of carpet for the church but not the color of worshipers' skin. God had already decided that.

The less I said that night and the more God said, the better things would go, I felt. Two biblical texts stuck in my mind: Joshua 24:15, which reads, "Choose you this day whom you will serve . . . , but as for me and my house, we will serve the LORD," and 1 John 4:20, which warns, "If someone says, 'I love God,' and hates his brother, he is a liar."

Standing floor level in front of the Lord's Supper Table, on which rested a suitcase-size pulpit Bible, I turned, took the massive Bible, held it before the people, and charged, "Let us choose this day whom we will serve, Christ or culture. But let us be truthful. Let us have a Bible that we will live by. If you choose culture over Christ this day, then I want you to come tear out this page that says we are to love one another, wad it up, and throw it away. If you choose to please your earthly father instead of your heavenly Father, then come rip out this page that reads, 'If someone says, I love God, and hates his brother, he is a liar.' Let's tear out and throw away all these pages we don't want in our Bible. Let's not be hypocrites. Let's make a Bible we will live by."

The sanctuary fell silent. "On the other hand," I continued, "if this day you choose Christ over culture, I want you to come up here, take this pulpit Bible from me, and seal your commitment by reading from this Book before God and this assembly. Choose you this day!"

With the charge complete, I sealed my own commitment to the Lordship of Jesus Christ by reading from 1 John 4:7-8: "Beloved, let us love one another, for love is from God, and everyone who loves is born of God and knows God. The one who does not love does not know God, for God is love." Eric Holleyman walked forward, took the Bible from me, faced the congregation, and began reading where I had stopped: "By this the love of God was manifested in us . . . ." He read until Kay marched down the aisle, received the huge Book from Eric, and read, "Beloved, if God so loved us, we also ought to love one another." Doug Taylor followed Kay. What a sight to behold! A Black man holding the pulpit Bible of Southern Baptist Church in

1979! "And this commandment we have from him, that the one who loves God should love his brother also," this child of God read.

Revival broke out! Miss Elsie Smith, one of our oldest widows, waddled forward and whispered in my ear, "Hon, I can't read; would you read for me?" Together we held the Bible as I read for her. Others came. Soon almost everyone had publicly declared their intentions to live according to God's will rather than man's ways.

Leon Johnson was the exception. Leon sat frozen on the back pew, a mask of hatred glued to his face. He rushed out into the night.

After everyone had left for the night, Kay, Doug, Eric, and I turned out the lights, locked up the church, and headed out the door. Before walking out into the black Southern night, not knowing what or who might be awaiting us, we prayed.

Relief! Crickets, not Klan, greeted us as we opened the door. We drove to the parsonage to change into casual clothes for the drive back to New Orleans. As we prepared to leave the parsonage, fear gripped us. Who would be waiting outside in the dark? We prayed together, then opened the door. Nothing! Praise the Lord, no one was there! Driving down the deserted country roads that carried us toward I-55 miles away, our pulse quickened each time headlights hit our rear-view mirror. Not until we drove into the bright lights of New Orleans did we feel safe.

When Eric, Kay, and I returned to the church field the next weekend, we were shocked. Southern Baptist Church was a ghost town! The Klan had reached the members during the week. Almost no one dared attend church. Kenny Joe Cobb, the leading tither in the church, said he'd never give another nickel as long as I was pastor of the church. Elmer Newton, the oldest deacon in the church, swore he'd never darken the door of the church as long as I was there. Despite our best efforts to shepherd the flock, visit the church families, preach the word, love the unlovely, visit the sick, the widows, and those confined to nursing homes, and pray, pray, pray, nothing worked. Our days at Southern Baptist Church were numbered.

After doing everything we could to rebuild the fellowship, I resigned as pastor of Southern Baptist Church. Six months of painful struggle came to an end. Kay and I simply felt that if the church were ever going to have a chance to heal and grow again, we needed to go. The loving thing for us to do was to leave.

I am told the first question the Pastor Search Committee asked each new pastoral candidate was, "What do you think of n—s in the church?"

And so it was in the 1950s, 1960s, and 1970s.

But this is a new millennium.

Or is it?

With Liberty and Justice for All

An attorney friend and I were lamenting inequity in justice and race issues in America when she mused, "If someone offered you 20 million dollars to become Black, would you do it?" The question struck with the force of a sledgehammer on a fly.

Any attempt to remove the question from my mind would prove the equivalent of seeking to remove wrinkles from cardboard. The question is provocative. Why? Because most White people I know would offer a resounding "No" to the query. And why is that? Because we know our society is racially biased.

We are, in 2021, sixty-seven years removed from the epochal *Brown v. Board of Education* decision rendered by the U.S. Supreme Court in 1954, which made segregation illegal in educational institutions. The firmly embedded "Separate but Equal" doctrine in American education was allegedly given a decent burial. Today, however, housing demographics, population shifts, and private academies have resulted in the net effect of reversing the court's decision. Sadly, K–12 education in much of America remains largely "separate and unequal."

We are, in 2021, fifty-seven years removed from the civil rights movement's Freedom Summer of 1964, where our American ideals of liberty, justice, and equality for all inspired voter registration drives and freedom schools in the Jim Crow South. To be sure, changes in our society have been nothing short of revolutionary. For that we can all be grateful.

Yet, more than a half-century later, one wonders if White supremacy remains rooted in the American psyche. Is there a racial caste system in America? In Michelle Alexander's *New York Times* bestseller, *The New Jim Crow: Mass Incarceration in the Age of Colorblindness*, the author argues that Jim Crow is alive and well and thriving in America's criminal justice system.[6]

A favorite folk protest song of the '60s lamented, "Where have all the soldiers gone?" Today, with 70 percent of African American women unmarried, we might protest too, asking, "Where have all the African American men gone?"[7] The answer? "Gone to prisons, every one." Okay, not every one, but too many.

Today, 1 of 3 African American males will serve jail time, in some cities 1 of 2. In some states Black men are sentenced to jail at a rate of twenty to fifty times greater than White males. Are stereotyping and racial profiling factors in this horror? What about the "war on drugs"? Research shows that White and Black use and selling of drugs occur at similar rates. Yet 49 percent of African American males will be arrested by the age of twenty-three for drug-related crimes. Alexander observes, "The United States imprisons a larger percentage of its black population than South Africa did at the height of apartheid." Ouch!

I have been unable to stop thinking about my friend's question. So I posed this question in a Facebook post: "With liberty, justice, and equality for all. Hmmm . . . . Really? If offered 20 million dollars to become Black, would you do it?"

The responses were sudden, passionate, and memorable. A local television station received calls and complaints, which, in turn, led to their interviewing me and running a segment on their evening news regarding "a racially charged Facebook post by Carson-Newman University President Randall O'Brien."

Opinions of me have ranged from lunatic, idiot, and racist to heroic. Although my emotions fluctuate with the epithets, none of

6. New York: New Press, 2012.

7. Diane Stewart, "Why are so few Black women married in America?" Marketplace.org, October 6, 2020 (https://www.marketplace.org/2020/10/06/why-are-so-few-black-women-married-in-america/).

that matters. What does matter, though, is that parts of our society are more offended by a post on the subject of racial inequality than they are about the injustice of inequality. Other people simply did not understand the essence of the question. (I am not sure which is most troubling.) Still others, thankfully, appreciated the call to conversation and lent encouraging support.

I confess I have other questions. Here's one: Why, as Martin Luther King Jr. once said, is 11:00 a.m. on Sunday the most segregated hour in Christian America?[8]

Must we remain "separate but equal" in worship? The church, we say, is called to be "the light of the world." Should that refer to taillights or headlights? Does the church suffer from laryngitis in the face of moral issues confronting religion and society? When will the invisible God become audible? Why are God's speakers speechless? What do we do with the haunting indictment of Romano Guardini, "The church is the cross on which Christ is crucified"?

What should we expect of our legislative, executive, and judicial leaders? In the Federalist Papers, No. 51, Madison wrote, "If men were angels, no government would be necessary. If angels were to govern men, neither external nor internal controls . . . would be necessary." Who will speak the truth to power? Who will ask the hard questions?

Seems to me we need criminal justice reform, educational system reform, and church reform. For this we'll need more than a hypothetical 20 million dollars and a controversial question.

But it's a start.

---

8. *Meet the Press*, April 17, 1960 (www.youtube.com/watch?v=1q881g1L_d8).

MUSINGS

Failure and Other Blessings

Who likes to fail? "Not I," said the Little Red Hen. Failure brings disappointment. Disappointment is the opposite of joy. Who wants to be unhappy? Thus, failure is anathema, a curse to our well-being . . . right? Not so fast, my fellow failures.

Failure? I know, I know. No one wants to be called a failure. I get that. But who among us hasn't failed? Where is she who hasn't suffered disappointment—in school, work, play, family, or other relationships? Haven't we all?

Might failure be a blessing in disguise? Not always, certainly, or even usually, but sometimes, perhaps?

To be sure, human development brings us to an early life stage of "Industry v. Inferiority" (in the words of Eric Erickson). Here we strive to master our tasks, then compare our ability to do so in relation to our friends and schoolmates. When we succeed in our challenges, we gain confidence. When we routinely fail, however, a sense of inferiority takes root. Feelings of competence and confidence are desirable; feelings of failure and inferiority are not. No one likes to fail. Thus, let us hasten to acknowledge the importance of success for a lifelong sense of well-being.

But is there any word regarding the value of *unexpected, intermittent failure*, however distasteful it may be to us?

Writer David Brooks of the *New York Times* observes, "Success leads to the greatest failure, which is pride. Failure leads to the greatest virtue, which is humility and learning."[9]

To be fair, true as Brooks's words may be, he cites an *unhealthy season of success that lies beyond confidence, while approving a healthy* stage of failure far short of deep-rooted inferiority. In other words, the provocateur presents success in an unfavorable light and failure in a favorable one. The nineteenth century French novelist Victor Hugo chose the same tact when he wrote, "Adversity makes men, and prosperity makes monsters."

We have all experienced painful opportunities to learn from defeat. Admittedly, not all of us take advantage of our occasions to learn from failure, nor do we embrace humility when it comes calling. Yet I dare say most of us do, wittingly or unwittingly.

Each of us could prepare a list of our failures in life. A few of my storied heartaches include failing to successfully romance the girl I had assumed I would marry, quitting my college basketball team, flunking out of college when I was nineteen, fighting in a misguided, catastrophic war in Southeast Asia, and being passed over for the presidency of my college alma mater. I'm sure you could add your own list.

Flannery O'Connor notes, "There is something in us, as storytellers and as listeners to stories, that demands the redemptive act, that demands that what falls at least be offered the chance to be restored."[10]

Agreed. In my case, my courtship failure led to my marriage to Kay, an angel on furlough from heaven. Country star Garth Brooks croons, "Sometimes I thank God for unanswered prayers. . . . 'Cause some of God's greatest gifts are unanswered prayers." Not a bad theologian, that Mr. Brooks.

"Adversity makes men," Hugo declared. Quitting the basketball team plagued me with guilt that made me never want to quit anything again. Flunking out of college humiliated me, driving me

---

9. *The Road to Character* (New York : Random House, 2015) xii.

10. *Mystery and Manners: Occasional Prose* (New York, Farrar, Straus & Giroux, 1969), 48.

to redeem myself by earning a doctoral degree and graduating from Yale with honors. Fighting in Vietnam built an unquenchable fire in my soul for peace and justice. Missing out on the presidency of my alma mater featured prominently in my availability for the executive vice presidency of Baylor University and, later, the presidency of Carson-Newman University, two "unbelievably believable" blessings of Providence.

Who likes to fail? No one I know.

But what if failure is not the end of the story?

Getting Leah

"What is this you have done to me?" Jacob asked Laban. "Was it not for Rachel that I served you?"

Jacob loved Rachel. He had worked seven years in exchange for Laban's younger daughter's hand in marriage. When the seven years of work was complete, Laban hosted a great wedding feast. Everyone made merry! Jacob celebrated his honeymoon. But "in the morning, behold, it was Leah!"

Alas, poor Jacob labored seven long years for Rachel but got Leah, Rachel's older sister. "Leah's eyes were weak, but Rachel was beautiful of form and face," says the storyteller in Genesis 29. "Jacob loved Rachel but hated Leah."

We all know what it's like to long for "Rachel" but "get Leah," don't we? Who among us hasn't failed or suffered disappointment?

What happens when we do everything in our power, work seven long years to "get Rachel"—whatever our Rachel may be—but for whatever reason, perhaps through no fault of our own, we "get Leah" instead?

First, shouldn't we stop and realize what it was like to *be* Leah? One young woman is pretty, and everyone notices and comments. Her sister, however, stands sadly to the side waiting for the compliment that never comes. Call her Leah. A little boy sits alone, heartbroken, again left out of games as sides are chosen. Color him Leah.

Thankfully, the consistent testimony of the Good Book is that the Lord is with the Leahs, siding with the outcasts, the oppressed, the poor, the broken, the "Leahs of these." While Rachel is yet barren, the story relays, Leah gives birth to five children, including four sons: Reuben, Simeon, Levi, and Judah. Embedded within their names, verb roots deliver a message. God *saw* Leah's affliction, *heard* her cries, *joined* in her struggle, and inspired her *praise*. The names say so. God blesses Leah.

And Jacob? What word is there for Jacob and for "Jacobs" everywhere? The fertility of blessing may not come to us in the "Rachels" of this world; it often comes in the "getting of Leah," in the struggles, failures, and disappointments of life.

When the genealogy of Christ is traced back through time, the messianic line runs through Abraham and Sarah, Isaac and Rebekah, Jacob and *Leah*. Not the desirable Rachel! Life's richest blessings often blossom from our disappointments and defeats—not through the glitter, glamor, and gold, and not from the golden ones, after all.

As a personal example, on December 1, 1969, the United States Selective Service conducted a lottery based on birthdays to determine the order of twenty-year-old young men to be drafted into the army, with the likelihood of being sent off to the Vietnam War. My birth date, August 29, was selected #61. This unlucky low number meant I would be drafted soon! One might say, "I had hoped for Rachel but got Leah."

Yet it was while serving in the army that I "found myself." For several preceding years I had struggled mightily with haunting questions all of us must answer: "Who am I?" "What's my purpose in life?" "What am I going to do with my life?" Before entering the military, I was a soul adrift without an anchor. During my army years, life's critical questions found answers. I came out whole.

Then, when the girl I loved and hoped to marry ended our relationship, I was devastated. I cried. Hurting all over during the painful loss, like Jacob, I felt I had "gotten Leah."

Little did I know the course my life would take. Meeting and marrying Kay brought one of my life's most glorious blessings. From the ashes of one of life's deepest disappointments grew the sweetest flower of my life.

One wonders, for those who have eyes to *see* her, for those who have ears to *hear* her, and for those who have arms to *embrace* her, might it not be, for Jacobs everywhere, that the most beautiful bride after all is Leah?

Joy to the World of Insects and Humans

Guess how many insects inhabit our planet? More than 200 million for every human being! With their number reaching as high as 10 quadrillion, Earth could be called "The Planet of Insects." We humans, if you count the ancestors of Homo sapiens, have been around roughly 2 million years; Homo sapiens have only been here for approximately 200,000-300,000 years. Insects, on the other hand, first appeared 479 million years ago!

Most insects have six legs and two sets of wings. They communicate well with each other, relying heavily on scent, sound, and sight. They use these to find a mate, secure food, and avoid their enemies or, in other words, to live and pass along their genes. Insects primarily smell through their antennae (some male butterflies can pick up the scent of a female several miles away). They hear through ears along their bodies, and they see with compound eyes, such as the triangular ones of a stinging wasp or the 30,000 eyes of the dragonfly. Having no lungs, insects breathe through holes on the sides of their bodies.

Honeybees can distinguish human faces from among portraits. They can also remember a face for at least two days. Female aphids give birth to their young without their eggs being fertilized. (Yes, this constitutes virgin birth!) In addition, although female honeybees are born from fertilized eggs, *male* honeybees are not. They are born from *unfertilized* eggs. They have no father!

As many as eighty taxonomic groups may experience virgin births. Along with female aphids and honeybees, these include sharks, reptiles, and lizards. No mammal, however, is known to have experienced asexual reproduction.

There is a story in the Bible about a baby boy being born without the participation of a human father.

Christians worldwide celebrate this birth each Christmas, and year-round as well.

Is "virgin birth" possible? For some species, we know the answer is "yes."

For humans?

That is the story of Christmas.

Mabel's Beauty Shop & Chain Saw Repair

Birmingham, Alabama, police are investigating the death of a man in his forties, fatally shot, authorities say, at Mabel's Beauty Shop & Chain Saw Repair.

Christian sympathy aside for a moment, how about the name of that establishment—*Mabel's Beauty Shop & Chain Saw Repair*. Some things just don't seem to go together well: tornadoes and mobile homes, gymnastics and geriatrics, flatulence and first dates, Grandma and a mustache, flying pigeons and bare heads, to name a few.

Odd combinations and their prohibitions date at least to Old Testament times: "Thou shalt not breed together two kinds of cattle; thou shalt not sow your field with two kinds of seed, nor wear a garment with two kinds of material mixed together" (Lev 19:19).

Then, of course, there is the famous New Testament passage, "Be not unequally yoked together with unbelievers" (2 Cor 6:14), which some apply to marriage. Equally or unequally yoked, married couples should love Mabel's. Where else might the perfect pair go, where she can get her hair done while he sharpens his chain?

Maybe church is kind of like Mabel's. One could conceivably go to church to show off one's coiffure, while the other sharpens their spiritual edge. Certainly, unlikely combinations abound among steeple people: sinners and saints, lost and found, dead and alive, blind who see, folks born again, rich who are poor and poor who are rich, last who are first and first who are last.

If we can't make it to Mabel's Beauty Shop & Chain Saw Repair this weekend, we could always give church a try. It might be safer, and we could even decide the purpose of our visit: to show off our coif or to sharpen our spiritual cutting edge.

Miss America Dreamin' in Vietnam

We all dreamed of making it home alive from Vietnam. Most of us made it. Many didn't. Until our dreams could come true, however, we looked forward to other morale boosts, R & R, mail from home, care packages from home, and Bob Hope USO shows.

Percentagewise, few of us in infantry ever had the opportunity to see a Bob Hope show in Nam.

But once I did.

For some reason—hopelessly lost in my geriatric memory—I found myself out of the bush for a few days at Camp Eagle, a base camp much larger than Camp Evans, from which our grunt battalion operated and received resupplies.

Topping my temporary good luck, the Bob Hope USO show played that very night in the camp. What a morale boost!

I arrived early.

Jim Nabors, Les Brown and His Band of Renown, and Dean Martin's Gold Diggers accompanied Hope on the tour. Hope's jokes, always a hit, brought roars of laughter. Gorgeous girls in miniskirts and go-go boots sent us GIs into dreamland.

Miss America 1971, Phyllis George (who later called the trip "the highlight of my reign")—and several state beauty pageant winners—accompanied the August '71 tour. Wolf whistles pierced the hot air. Hope's comedy act played easily on GI hormones, bringing waves of laughter and sustained applause. Music rocked the festive stage.

For me, the highlight of the show came after it was over. Miss America spotted me down front in the crowd after the performance, knelt on the edge of the stage, and asked, "What's your name?"

"O'Brien. Randall O'Brien."

"Where are you from, Randall?"

"McComb, Mississippi."

"I'm from Texas. Close to your home state. Can I autograph your steel pot?"

"Yes, ma'am. I voted for you."

Now, I ask you: why would Phyllis George select the handsomest, most rugged, intelligent, well-built man present? I don't know; I reckon Miss Americas can dream, too.

Running Bare

After processing into "the service" on March 24, 1970, and receiving the infamous onion-head haircut, vaccinations, olive-drab fatigues, socks, cap, underwear, belt, and black boots, this "boot camp" fell hard on our backs. For eight weeks, from April 2 to May 29, Army drill sergeants owned us . . . some might say abused us.

Fort Bragg, North Carolina, is a long way away from home—in a lot of ways. I had my share of homesickness, but this was a time to find out what I was made of, and I knew it.

Handling well the physical aspects of the grueling training regimen at 5 feet 10 inches, 150 pounds, I at times dropped back behind the platoon to help anemic, faint, nice-guy Jerry Antone (name changed) complete our five-mile runs or ten-mile forced marches with heavy rucksacks. Drill Sergeant Arenas screamed obscenities mercilessly in Antone's face as the poor boy wobbled behind the platoon, trying in vain to keep up. Sergeant Arenas yelled at me, too, for intervening, but I paid no attention, holding Antone up, running along with him. Though he would never show it, Drill Sergeant Arenas must have liked what he saw.

When several of the drill sergeants stayed out post-midnight, drinking to excess, boasts floated freely with bets following.

"Wake up! O'Brien, wake up!" Drill Sergeant Arenas shook me.

"Huh? Sir? What? What!"

"Put your boots on and come with me!"

"My boots?"

"Yes, your boots! Put 'em on and come with me!"

Taken to an open field nearby, I saw another drill sergeant standing in the crisp moonlit night, waiting with one of his trainees.

Each drill sergeant was inebriated. Lining us up like racehorses and waving money, their cussing, boastful bets cracked the cold night air. My fellow boots- and underwear-clad opponent glanced my way. Our eyes spoke fear. “Can’t lose; these guys are crazy!”

“O’Brien, you run like a sumbi*ch!”

“Yes sir.”

“Don’t call me sir! I work for a living!”

“Yes sir, I mean, yes, drill sergeant!”

“You better not let that *&^%* beat you! You hear me?”

“Yes, drill sergeant!”

“Get on your mark! Get set! *Go!*”

We were off! Down there and back! Skint-head GIs in underwear raced in the moonlight to the cussing commands and cheers of their drunken handlers; it must have been a hilarious sight. I felt sorry for the other guy. But not *that* sorry! I couldn’t lose. He couldn’t, either.

Maybe the other poor guy was still half-asleep. But this was one time when my long nose came in handy; that’s what I won by. Twice.

With profanity aplenty, paper money flew between hands. Game over. I returned to bed, slipping into the barracks quietly. Drill Sergeant Arenas never said a word about that night.

At the end of basic training, he nominated me for the Leadership Award. Is that how it works? Was I the most deserving? I wonder how many prizes in other fields and organizations are awarded through ingratiation.

I wonder.

Sisyphus and the Peasant

Our neighbors call me Sisyphus. At least they do during the growing season of spring and summer. Our heavily shaded front yard cannot grow grass. The lawn is beautiful, featuring several varieties of trees, shade-preferring flowers, hasta, ferns, shrubs, benches, an arbor, bird baths, winding stone paths, and manicured ground cover. But no grass. In addition to a soft covering of mulch, alas, a pesky weed variety of vine threatens to take over our grounds and ruin our garden of Eden.

In Greek mythology, Sisyphus is sentenced by Zeus to everlasting fruitless labor. His curse is to roll a stone up a mountain only to have the boulder roll back down the steep incline. Sisyphus must retrieve the rock and push it up the hill again. And again. And again. And again. The nightmare never ends. Futile, cruel, endless labor characterizes the poor man's eternal fate.

"How's Sisyphus today?" our neighbors tease. It seems my incessant attempts to control the irrepressible spreading weed cast me unwillingly in the role of the Greek character. Perhaps the neighbors are right. Continuously, futilely weed-eating, I do feel sentenced to watch the undying growth reappear as though it was pruned to spread widely.

"Woe is me! What did I do to deserve this fate?"

"Why don't you spray your yard with root-killing chemicals?"

"Because I like my trees. Besides, I'd rather have weeds than cancer."

"Makes sense. Okay, well, back to your rolling stones, Sisyphus."

Camus argues that life is like this: sheer absurdity! "We're all Sisyphus," he says. We work. Eat. Sleep. Arise. Eat. Work. Sleep. Work some more. Monday, Tuesday, Wednesday, Thursday, Friday, and sometimes Saturday and Sunday, too. Rolling that stone up the mountain. Our is a monotonous, meaningless, torturous life, he asserts.

Maybe. Maybe not.

A peasant wandered here and yon. Across the land, over the plains, and by the sea he roamed. Scaling hills, treading paths, and walking valleys, he traveled. Knowing no home, sleeping under the stars or in caves, wherever invited, he ate fish, olives, bread, then fasted, ate fish, olives, bread, then fasted, ate fish, olives, bread, then fasted . . . .

Camus never called the peasant Sisyphus. No one else did either. Meaningless life? Hardly!

Alienation, not monotony, is the problem of human existence, writes Fromm. Estranged from each other, we waste away "in the dungeon of our aloneness." Love helps us escape. Love changes everything, removing the curse of alienation, making us one with all. The peasant believed the same thing. In fact, he believed it first.

"Love God and each other," said the peasant. Love life, self, nature, enemies, world. Embrace rather than resist. Love alone converts meaninglessness into meaning, common ground into holy ground, work into worship, complaint into call, the mundane into miracle, enemies into friends, resentment into renewal, and weeds into wonder.

"Let the weeds grow with the wheat," said the peasant. "The day will come when they're separated" (Matt 13:24-30).

Sounds good to me. Maybe I should till my garden and be glad not sad, grateful not hateful, for the fullness of Mother Earth. Perhaps I should flow not fight. Enjoy not endure. Work not worry. Let go, let God. Find beauty in my duty.

Caregiving is always meaningful, never meaningless. To whom should we strive to be compared, Sisyphus or the peasant?

"Let him who is without meaning roll the last stone."

What's It All About, Alfie?

For the 1966 romantic comedy movie titled *Alfie*, starring Michael Caine as a self-centered womanizer, Burt Bacharach and Hal David contributed the title song. Borrowing a line from the movie, their song begins, "What's it all about, Alfie?" adding, "Is it for the moment we live?"

Haven't we all asked that question in a myriad of ways? What *is* life all about? The song continues, "What's it all about when you sort it out, Alfie? Are we meant to take more than we give?"

Sigmund Freud argues that we humans are moved by a "will to pleasure." Frederick Nietzsche and Alfred Adler claim that we are moved by a "will to power." Viktor Frankl states that we find our hope in a "will to meaning." T. S. Eliot allows that we all want to feel important. Jesus promotes unselfish love, adding, "It is better to give than to receive." Eric Fromm believes that "Love is the answer to the problem of human existence." Archibald Macleish posits, "Love is all there is." Qoheleth, the writer of Ecclesiastes, says it's all futile, "vanity of vanities." Having tried to center his life on wisdom first, pleasure next, then work, power, and finally wealth, he determines, "It's all in vain." Only the worship of God makes sense, he concludes.

What say you? What's it all about, Alfie?

Is it too simplistic to suggest that the world is divided between "givers and grabbers"? Certainly. But is one approach right and the other wrong? What's wrong with desiring to grab a little pleasure or power or wealth or meaning? Does that make one a narcissist? Or a materialist? Or an Epicurean? Or a cynic? Doesn't life consist of both giving and receiving? Of course it does.

Many of us have learned, however, that life fixated on self-indulgence leaves one wondering, "Is this all there is?" To be sure, Maslow's hierarchy of needs is basic to all of us, including the following: oxygen, food, water, sleep, sex, rest, and excrement, along with safety and security needs, love and belonging, respect given and received, self-esteem, morality, problem-solving ability, and self-actualization. Our needs must be met. Our "wants" may also be pursued. Yet a self-centered existence proves meaningless for many of us, leaving self-acceptance and self-esteem unrealized.

Most of us, perhaps all of us, desire to be great, important, famous, and loved. The majority of us, of course, will not be famous, as much as we may wish to be.

Despite delicious ego gratification, famous artists, actors, writers, musicians, athletes, politicians, and others may feel enormous pressure to please their public by performing always at laudatory levels. My guess is they do.

But imagine the despair that some, many, or most of us feel in painting our art no one will see, penning poems no one will read, writing songs no one will sing, or playing music no one will hear. What is it like to wear perfume no one will smell, dream dreams no one will share, extend hands no one will hold, or think thoughts no one will care about?

Some of us know. Loneliness, despair, and depression hurt and even kill, don't they?

Fromm's diagnosis of the human dilemma strikes me as right: "The deepest need of man, then, is the need to overcome his separateness, to leave the prison of his aloneness." If Fromm's diagnosis is correct, however, so is his prescription: "Love, [is] the answer to the problem of human existence."[11] Unselfish love.

"It's better to give than to receive," said Jesus. He did not imply, though, that receiving is bad. He accepted material gifts as well as

---

11. *Art of Loving* (New York: Harper & Row, 1962), 8.

affection from others. The teacher simply stressed that it is *better* to give than to receive.

Interesting. A life oriented toward helping others paradoxically ensures help for oneself. Ironically, pleasure—meaning joy, peace, and fulfillment—results not from self-indulgent pursuit but rather as a byproduct of giving oneself for the welfare of others.

Our question proves central to human existence: "What's it all about, Alfie?" Responding to the universal question Bacharach and David soulfully put to music, two other renowned songwriters, Lennon and McCartney, beautifully sang our answer: "All you need is love."

Why Evil, Ponders a Five-year-old Child

When our son, Kris, was five years old, he sought the answer to a burning question: "How did the devil get alive?"

"No one really knows for sure," I tried, "but the answer most often given is—"

"Why doesn't God just kill the devil?" Kris interjected. "Wouldn't that help make it better?"

Kris's question requires a response.

A war raged in Rwanda, taking the lives of countless children during Kris's fifth year. "Does God like that, Momma?" Kris probed.

"No, honey, God does not like that at all."

"Then why doesn't He stop it?"

"God wants us to work to do that."

"When Daddy gets home, I'll tell him. He'll stop it."

"Well, he'd want to, I'm sure."

"My dad was in the army. He'll get his gun and stop it."

Familial flattery aside, Kris's dad tried that once, in Vietnam. It didn't work. Alexander Solzhenitsyn, Russian philosopher and novelist, writes, "If only there were evil people . . . committing evil deeds, and it were necessary only to separate them from the rest of us and destroy them. But *the line dividing good and evil cuts through the heart of every human being*."

Evil, unfortunately, has plagued human existence since the beginning and will continue to plague us until the end, which likely will come about due to our evil designs. In the meantime, how shall we live? Tolstoy observes, "Everyone thinks of changing the world, but no one thinks of changing himself."

Convicting. What if we all embraced the Golden Rule? Dating back at least as far as Confucius, 500 years before Christ, these wise words of justice, peace, and love appear conceptually in Christianity, Buddhism, Hinduism, Judaism, Taoism, and all of the world's major religions: *Do unto others as you would have them do unto you.*

Living these words of wisdom promises to help us reduce evil and advance peace on earth and goodwill toward all. For this hope we should all be thankful, whether age five or ninety-five. Right, Kris?

GRATITUDE

A Leper in Waco

The story is told of the leper who was healed of his disease. One of ten disfigured people made well that day by the itinerant miracle worker, he was the only one to return to thank the faith healer. "Were not ten cleansed? But the nine—where are they?" asked Jesus, the healer.

When stories are told, we often find our place within them, identifying with one character or another. Confession time: I am embarrassed to say that I relate to the nine. Far too often, I take for granted blessings, goodwill, bigheartedness, and countless benefits bestowed upon me. Favor, good fortune, godsends abound in my life. Yet, far too many times, I number among the nine who never take the time to be thankful or to express it even if I am. In fact, the opposite is often true. Frequently, I am an ingrate, sometimes negative, critical, resentful, or unaware of my blessings. One can be healed of physical leprosy and still suffer from spiritual leprosy. As with families and communities affected by rotted flesh in other times, no one today wants to be around someone infected with a diseased spirit.

I was contagious one particular day and knew it. It was a Saturday in Waco, Texas. Baylor University Law School, where I served as provost, was hosting its commencement exercise, a celebration event. I cannot declare why I was in a negative, depressed state of mind, because I do not know why. I just was. The occasion, I am ashamed to say, was one I planned to endure rather than enjoy. I was miserable.

The president of the university, the dean of the law school, and I, the provost, were gathered for a photograph with the graduating class. In my foul mood, I was placed between two young women lawyers-to-be. On my left stood a beautiful young woman, Maggie Weaver, wearing a wig to cover her bald head. The class knew that Maggie was terminally ill with cancer. She looked at me, smiled broadly, and said, "I am so grateful to have lived long enough to be here today to graduate! My dream was to finish law school and I did it!"

On my right, positioned in her wheelchair, sat Allison Dickson, a student I had taught, who had suffered with muscular dystrophy since shortly after birth. She was a quadriplegic, unable to move 95 percent of her small body. She finished first in her class. As she lifted a finger to push a button to roll her wheelchair closer to me while the photographer lined us all up, Allison looked up at me, eyes sparkling, and said, "I love you."

"But the nine—where are they?" Jesus asked. For one bright, sunshining moment, one day, one memory, I was no longer among them.

An Unexpected Blessing

It was "one of those days."

In trying to fly from Texas to Florida, I missed one plane and had to motor to a different city an hour and a half away to catch another plane, only to find that plane delayed five hours. Hoping to make my niece's wedding rehearsal and dinner in Ocala, I arrived late in Orlando, still an hour-and-fifteen-minute drive via rental car. Adding to my hard luck, I had no change for the multiple toll roads, only credit cards, which are unacceptable at the toll booths. I missed the rehearsal and dinner. I did, however, receive a call from our eighteen-year-old son back home. Water pipes had burst and water was everywhere in our home. "One of those days," indeed!

Disappointed and weary, I found a hotel for the night. Awaiting me in my room appeared these words:

> In ancient times, there was a prayer for "The Stranger Within our Gates." Because this inn is a human institution to serve people, and not solely a money-making organization, we hope God will grant you peace and rest while you are under our roof.
>
> May this room and inn be your "second home." May those you love be near you in thoughts and dreams. Even though we may not get to know you, we hope that you will be as comfortable and happy as if you were in your own home.
>
> May the business that brought you our way prosper. May every call you make and every message you receive add to your joy. When you leave, may your journey be safe.

> We are all travelers. From birth until death we travel the eternities. May these days be pleasant for you, profitable for society, helpful for those you meet, and a joy to those who know and love you best.

All blessings are good. The unexpected ones may be best. Thank you, Holiday Inn Express, Ocala, Florida! The wedding was as beautiful as your blessing.

I Once Had a Friend

We were born next door to each other, in rent houses, to working-class parents who labored long and hard to pull themselves and their children up with them to middle-class status. When, in time, the goal was achieved, our families bought houses a block apart.

He and I attended the same schools in the same grades for twelve years. We both played sports, baseball, basketball, and football being our favorites. He was bigger, stronger, and faster than I. Smarter, too. A great student in all subjects.

In the school yard, he always picked me to be on his team. As we grew older, we played on city league teams, sometimes on the same team, sometimes against each other. The latter never worked out well for me.

His family prospered somewhat more than ours, though neither did much, really. In elementary school he bought me candy after school at the unpainted corner store, where the proprietors lived upstairs. Our favorites? Orange wax whistles, Red Hots, and NuGrape sodas.

We would walk to his house after school and watch Batman on TV. Later, in our teen years, we listened to rock 'n' roll records on his family's stereo set and watched Dick Clark's *American Bandstand*. He was a good dancer. I was not.

The onslaught of puberty catapulted us to the downtown Palace movie theater, where he paid my way to see and fall in love with Haley Mills in *Pollyanna* and sit in awe of Sean Connery as Agent 007—Bond, James Bond—in *Goldfinger*. We idolized the Fab Four in *A Hard Day's Night*, and—how shall I say this—identified hormonally with Dustin Hoffman in his garden of temptation with Mrs. Robinson in *The Graduate.*

When I could not possibly afford the mandatory navy blue blazer for high school basketball team travel, he quietly decided not to play high school basketball and then lent me his blazer for the season.

He got me on his church basketball team, his independent league basketball team, and his fastpitch softball teams. When you're good enough, you can bring a friend.

We enjoyed countless spend-the-nighters. He'd tell me about his dates. As Most Valuable Back on our high school football team, dates with pretty girls seemed plentiful for him.

We shared countless suppers with his family, who treated me like a second son and brother. Sometimes he and I would play guitar and sing as if we were John and Paul.

Years later when I fought in Vietnam, he wrote me letters. When I attended Yale, he wrote me letters. After I left home, married, and had a family, he wrote me letters. When I came home for holidays, he came to see me at my parents' home. We would watch football bowl games, eat boiled peanuts, laugh, and tell thirty- and forty-year-old yarns.

He died far too young, at age fifty-seven, a victim of high blood pressure and a deadly stroke. Part of me died, too.

I remember well all these things. But what I remember most is how much he loved me. I loved him.

I am thankful for an endless list of blessings in my life. One of the sweetest is to have had a friend like Gary Boyd.

Knowing a Great Deal When I Hear One

"I don't like the thought of going through life without you," I whimpered to Kay one beautiful Saturday in October, two years and nine months after meeting her in college; both of us now navigating graduate school.

"That's so sweet," she responded.

"I don't know what to do about it."

"Well, some people decide to get married."

"Yeah, I reckon. But would you *do* that?"

"I don't know; I haven't been asked."

"Would you marry me?"

"Are you asking?"

"Yes, I guess I am."

"You guess?"

"No, I am. Shoot, I don't know how to do this. Will you marry me?"

"Yes. But you'll have to ask my daddy."

We traveled to Kay's home in the farmlands of Sunflower County in the Mississippi Delta. First thing I noticed? His hands were the size of shovels. Hard as anvils.

"How'd it go?" Kay asked later.

Speaking for both her mother and himself, her father had said to me, "Look, you're ugly. We don't like you or your long hair. You didn't grow up here and you don't know squat about farming or cattle; probably don't know the front end of a tractor from the back end. Think we get ham from a bushhog. You bear your shame for fighting in Vietnam, you and your fellow hippies. There's nothing you can ever do, now or in the future, to change our opinion of you. But if you can accept the fact that, for Kay's sake, we will tolerate—not like but *tolerate*—you hanging around our daughter, welcome to the family."

"What'd you say?"

"I thought that was a great deal. So I took it!"

Records Are Made to Be Corrected

"Read the list," Captain Wynn Wilson barked to his orderly as I stood in line facing him at Camp Evans, South Vietnam, December 8, 1971. Several of us soldiers were receiving our medals at the end of our tour of duty before stuffing them in our duffle bags and heading toward the bird waiting to fly us "back to the world."

"Combat Infantryman's Badge. Vietnam Service Medal, with Four Bronze Service Stars, United States Air Medal. Republic of Vietnam Campaign Medal with Device. Overseas Medal. Republic of Vietnam Gallantry Cross Unit Citation with Palm Device. Bronze Star," the junior serviceman read.

After awarding the other medals, Captain Wilson paused, puzzled, looked around, and asked, "Where's O'Brien's Bronze Star?"

"I don't know, sir," replied the orderly. "Hasn't arrived with paperwork yet, I guess, sir."

Turning back to look at me, Captain Wilson said, "O'Brien, I'm gonna give you an option."

"Yes sir!"

"You can 'fall out,' go get some shut-eye, write some letters, get some hot mess, and relax a few days 'til we get this straightened out."

"What's option 2, sir?"

"Option 2 is I put this unassigned Bronze Star in your hand, look you in the eye, say, 'Well, done, soldier,' and you go get your ass on that plane and go home to see Momma!"

"I'll take option 2, sir!"

I knew I had earned the medal. Why did I need a piece of paper saying I had? I was going home in time for Christmas and was so excited! I had survived Vietnam! Nothing else mattered.

Twenty-five years later, I handed my Bronze Star to Brenda Travis, a courageous teenage civil rights heroine who, in 1961, "sat in" in my hometown of McComb, Mississippi. For her heroism, she was sentenced to Reform School, then exiled from the state by the governor. Her bravery exceeds anything I have ever done. She deserves the medal far more than I!

As I grow old, children and grandchildren ask questions about the war. It dawns on me that if any of them, or future descendants, should research my army records, no official mention of the Bronze Star exists. Hindsight is 20/20, but a little delayed gratification back in 1971 would have served me well in the long run. Instead, a Bronze Star gift-wrapped in paperwork history was left behind out of preference for an earlier trip home. Did I make a mistake?

Are you ready for this? Synchronicity: Carl Jung defines the term as "meaningful coincidences." Kay and I moved from Baylor University in Texas to accept the presidency of Carson-Newman University in Tennessee. Of all the cities and states in America where Nam Captain Wynn Wilson might live, guess where he resides? Synchronicity! He grew up in New Market, Tennessee (population 1,369), four miles from Carson-Newman. *Unbelievable!* Captain Wilson now resides one hour away in Oliver Springs. What a reunion!

Soon, retired Captain Wilson and current Army Lieutenant Colonel Steve Howe, head of CNU's ROTC program, began actively seeking to have my army records corrected. Colonel Lance Oskey of Fort Knox, Kentucky, head of all regional ROTC programs, joined in the process, as did Congressman John J. "Jimmy" Duncan (R-TN) and his chief of staff, Vietnam veteran Bob Griffitts. This all-star lineup of determined, highly regarded, never-say-die men on mission cleared every hurdle and scaled every mountain of paperwork over a two-year period until their indefatigable, altruistic efforts on my behalf met with hallelujah success!

On the evening of September 10, 2018, forty-seven years after my tour of duty ended in Vietnam, a United States Army Bronze Star

Medal Presentation Dinner was given in my honor on the campus of Carson-Newman University. Congressman Duncan presented me a United States flag that had flown over the nation's Capitol. Congressman Duncan and Colonel Oskey presented the Bronze Star authorized by the Secretary of the Army, Mark Esper. Lt. Colonel Howe delivered an invocation. Captain Wilson spoke, as did I, expressing my eternal gratitude to all who made the records correction and the evening possible.

As emotionally moving as the evening proved for Kay and me, none of the fanfare had been a wish of mine. From the beginning, my only desire was for the United States Army to reflect accurately my Vietnam War record. The Congressman's Office and the United States Army, however, insisted on the public presentation.

The evening was one of grace, not merely merit, as they claim. The most memorable grace for me, though, are the two years of hard, relentless, time-consuming work on my behalf by Lt. Colonel Howe, Captain Wilson, Colonel Oskey, Congressman Duncan, and Chief of Staff Bob Griffitts. I will never forget them. For their friendship, character, influence, diligence, perseverance, and sacrificial labor of love on my behalf, I will forever be grateful.

And, of course, as they taught me, I am most grateful that records, like mistakes, are made to be corrected.

HARD TIMES

Charlie's Pen and Pencil Set

A dear friend of mine, a minister, died by suicide. I feel horrible. How hard was his life that I didn't know? How deep was his depression? Why did I not see? Could I not have, should I not have, made a lifesaving difference in his life? What kind of friend am I?

Despondent, I tell Kay where I'm going. I throw a bag in my car, pull out of the driveway, and motor to my friend's small hometown en route to his larger city of ministry and place of burial. Arriving, I find the sad news casting a pall over the village. Folks know. I park and walk down main street. Sadness hovers.

I pay for a haircut. Buy a suit of clothes next door at Simmons's Men's Store. Run into an old friend on the street, elderly Mr. Russell Bridges. "Sure sad about our friend, isn't it?"

"Yes sir, sure is," I manage.

"What are you doing here, anyway, Randall?"

"Just driving down for the funeral. Thought I'd swing through is all. Think I'm a little depressed. I just don't understand, Mr. Bridges."

"Randall, did I ever tell you about Charlie Lindsey?"

"No sir. Don't believe you did."

"Well, Charlie's dead now. Died a few years back. Old. Broken. Tired. Drunk a lot."

"Oh, okay."

"Every day of Charlie's life he bought a newspaper. First thing, every morning, he'd buy that paper. Carried it in his back pocket all day long. Had a nice pen and pencil set he carried in his front shirt pocket. Everywhere he went he carried that newspaper and pen and pencil set. But Randall, Charlie Lindsey couldn't read or write."

"You're kidding."

"No, I'm not kidding."

I catch on. My deceased friend was a minister whose own pain was camouflaged by his caring for the pain of others. But the story of Charlie Lindsey is bigger than that. I mean, isn't that all of us in some way? We're all Charlie Lindsey, aren't we?

To what extent do we go to hide our pain? To what extreme do we go to conceal our inadequacies, our hurts, our needs? And where does that road lead?

Dumb, Dumber, Dumbest

"Life is hard. It's even harder when you're stupid." So goes the saying. If we're honest, we'll all admit we've done some, shall we say, less than bright things. Once I wheeled my car through a gasoline service station in a fast U-turn, caught the looped gas pump hose with my left rear bumper, and pulled the pump out of the concrete, spraying gasoline all over the lot.

On another occasion, on the Saturday of our family's garage sale, I volunteered to drive to our bank before it closed at noon. Approximately $400 earned from the hard work of my wife and daughters would be safely deposited that day if I arrived in time. Presto, I made it! The money did not. Yours truly had placed the bag on the car trunk for some unknown reason, forgotten to retrieve it and put it in the car, and then backed out of the drive, motored away, and lost the money speeding along the boulevard.

So who am I to nominate my fellow geniuses for the epithets "Dumb, Dumber, and Dumbest"? Ah, why let a little hypocrisy spoil the fun?

Police arrested Lisa D. Duncan in a Florida city on a Friday night after she ran a red light, immediately drawing the attention of the arresting officers. Authorities report Duncan had a twenty-four-pack of Busch beer tightly secured with a seat belt while her sixteen-month-old passenger rode unrestrained. Ms. Duncan faces charges of child abuse, driving without a license, driving under the influence, and possession of drug paraphernalia. With her beer belted in but not the baby, should Duncan face an additional charge of the crime of *dumb*?

Fred and Red Smith, brothers in a New England state, found an eighty-pound semiprecious gem. The brothers argued about sly ways of selling the valuable stone without drawing attention to themselves. They decided to chop the gem into small pieces. Their clever idea diminished the price of the morganite crystal from 1 million dollars to less than $60,000! Wasn't there a movie about two guys titled "Dumb and *Dumber*?"

Johnny James Johnson, manager of a Jack in the Box restaurant in a quiet California town, reported that the store had been robbed after closing one night. The thief had taken $307 and fled. Johnson gave police sketch artist Thomas Calhoun a detailed description of the suspect. When Calhoun finished his drawing, he looked at it closely, then at Johnson, then back down at his work, then back at Johnson again. The picture looked like Johnson. When questioned, Johnson confessed.

"Life is hard; it's even harder when you're stupid," goes the saying. If pressed, I imagine most of us could confess embarrassing *personal* testimonial support for the adage, could we not? Nevertheless, should Hollywood ever decide to produce a movie titled, "Dumb, Dumber, *Dumbest*," we may have just stumbled upon three humble contenders for the hard-luck cast. Reckon?

(Names changed in the stories to protect the guilty.)

I Filled Up the Bag in the Airplane

Some things you don't have to tell. They just get found out. Who told Bill Maxey, anyway? I didn't. Maybe it was Randy Turner. He knew. How? One lazy afternoon inside his college dorm room he figured it out.

Randy and I were relaxing, talking about who-knows-what, when firecrackers left the hand of a prankster to slide devilishly under Randy's door. The blasts sent me diving over a bed, hitting the floor, shouting, "Get down! Get down!"

Randy's spontaneous laughter at my assumed humorous response ceased quickly when he saw I was shaken and embarrassed. Apologies erupted from each of us. But soon he knew.

It wasn't long before guys were asking, "What was Vietnam like?"

"It was like hell."

"Ever kill anybody?"

"Killed a lot of mosquitoes."

"Ever get shot?"

"Tried not to. Most o' the blood I shed was to leeches."

"How long were you there?"

"Tour of Duty."

"What branch?"

"Army."

"What'd ya do?"

"Tried to survive."

"I mean, what was your job?"

"Airborne Infantry, Air Assault."

"Wow! If you ever wanna tell us about it, I'd love to hear it."

"Not much to tell, really; but thanks, I'll remember that."

Eventually, I did loosen up and tell a few tales, most of which I'd never heard 'til I told 'em. Why not be a hero, right? Right. After all, I had tried to be humble. Maybe it's okay to look a little "Big Stuff." Then along comes Bill Maxey one day. "Hey, O'Brien, guess what? I told Dad about your Air Medal for aerial assault in Vietnam."

"You did?"

"Yeah, he is so excited!"

"'Bout what?"

"He wants to take you up in his plane. Can you go Saturday?"

"This Saturday?"

"Yeah, he's ready 'n' rarin'!"

"Yeah, sure. I guess so. Okay."

Now, why'd I agree to that?

It must have been somewhere between the fourth and fifth nose-dive, or straight-up climb, or wing roll, or who-knows-what-else, that Mr. Vietnam War Vet tossed his cookies. I had felt the nausea coming. Getting hot and sweaty, hoping to hold on.

"Y'all ever have to maneuver like this over there?" Mr. Maxey shouted, then banked sharply to the right and dropped off a tabletop, leaving my stomach forty feet to the left and above my head on the plane's ceiling.

"God, let him land this plane before I . . . ." Too late! Light green face. Perspiration. Cold sweat. Eureka! I filled up the bag in the backseat. Bill and his father up front heard it. Smelled it. Landed that plane quickly.

"Are you all right?"

Don't you hate it when the mask slides off? When the hero's mantle won't stay on? When your Audie Murphy persona flops to Barney Fife mode?

I can't speak for anybody else and wouldn't try, but my experience is that it's hard to impress others while you're barfing in a bag.

Let's Give It Another Shot

Michael and Bonnie Martin were having marriage problems. Nothing new there. Mrs. Martin had filed for divorce three times in the past nine years, the last coming only two months prior. The couple decided the union was worth saving. So they made a commitment to go for marriage counseling.

Mrs. Martin arrived first at St. James Episcopal Cathedral. Mr. Martin showed up late drinking a beer. Apparently, the counseling session was not going well. The Martins' counselor, the Reverend Russell Willingham, shared, "They were arguing. It was your typical domestic dispute. Then the fireworks started."

Matthew Yi of the Associated Press reports what happened next:

> With a beer in one hand and a gun in the other, Michael Martin shot his wife as she tried to walk out of the meeting at the church, their counselor said. A bleeding Bonnie Martin pulled a pistol from her purse and shot her husband in the shoulder. The two took the gun battle outside, where Mrs. Martin collapsed and was fired on again. Martin allegedly hit his wife at least once more before he ran out of bullets.[12]

Most of us have heard of all kinds of shots: flu shots, buckshot, booster shots, bad shots, good shots, hot shots, bank shots, snapshots, crack shots, pot shots, long shots, random shots, jump shots,

---

12. *Waco Tribune-Herald*, April 24, 1998, 6A.

free shots, big shots, and mug shots. But until now, have we ever heard of marriage counseling gunshots? Not I.

Clearly no shots from Cupid's bow, the tragic Martin gunfire lends all new meaning to the song "Double Shot of My Baby's Love."

"It's a good thing that he had been drinking," said the Reverend, "because he could have hit her more. He was a lousy shot."

Maybe so. But my guess is a lot of nerves were shot, including the Reverend's. I'm pretty sure this is not what the Reverend had in mind when he reminded the couple of their wedding vows, "until death do us part."

Mr. and Mrs. Martin were each admitted to the local hospital for treatment of their wounds. Police are filing attempted murder charges against both. If, however, through some miraculous turn of events, the couple evades prison time and chooses to give marriage one more shot, this time they might try the Bible, not bullets in church, especially where the Good Book counsels, "Husbands, love your wives; wives, respect your husbands."

Some might say the admonition is a long shot for the Martins' marriage. Maybe so. On the other hand, perhaps they're ready to give each other another shot.

Momma Said There'd Be Days Like This

How difficult could it be to fly from Waco, Texas, to Ocala, Florida, for my niece's wedding?

"Mr. O'Brien, you cannot board the plane with two bags."

"Oh, no ma'am, I don't want to carry my bags on; I want to check them."

"Sir, it's too late to check your bags for this flight. You can carry one bag on."

"But I have two bags."

"You can't carry two bags on."

"But if I can't check my bags, and I can't carry them on . . . ."

"That's right. You'll have to take a later flight. I can put you on standby for the 12:30 flight to Dallas."

"Is it full?"

"Yes."

"So I would have to wait three hours but still might not get on the flight?"

"That is correct. But if someone didn't show, you'd get their seat."

"But I have a connecting flight in Dallas."

"Well, you could drive to Dallas."

"I don't want to drive to Dallas. I paid for a flight to Dallas."

"Well, you could catch a limo."

"That's still not flying. Anyway, I don't want to pay twice to get to Dallas."

"What if we pay for the limo?"

"What kind of limo?"

"That white stretch limousine sitting out front?"

"You're kidding; not a panel van?"

"No sir. The Real Deal."

"And you're paying?"

"Yep."

"I'll take it."

***

"May I have your attention, please? All ticket holders for American Airlines Flight 482 to Orlando! American Airlines Flight 482 to Orlando has been moved to Gate 18. We will be experiencing a brief delay."

Brief delay? Arriving in Orlando five hours later, I call Kay, who has flown down two days prior to help with final wedding preparations. "Hon, we just now landed in Orlando, and I still need to get my baggage, rent a car, and drive the hour and fifteen minutes to Ocala. Since the rehearsal dinner is starting in a few minutes, I don't think I can make it."

"Well, try. Maybe you can get here before it ends, anyway. If not, we'll understand. Oh, and hon, you will need change for the toll roads."

Having given most of my cash to our son, Kris, to buy meals while we were away, and having tipped the limo driver any bills I had left, my total available cash for the toll roads was exactly zero. No problem. Debit card and ATM to the rescue!

"Insufficient funds available," read the screen.

"Hmmm. After eating Chinese food for lunch in the DFW airport food court, then purchasing Walter Isaacson's *Einstein: His Life and Universe*, for thirty-two dollars, apparently I have less than forty dollars remaining in my account," I reasoned. So I tried again, this time requesting twenty instead of forty.

"Insufficient funds available," taunted the monitor.

"Good gracious! Am I that low? Shoulda moved some money over from my other account. I'll try something else."

Drove to a Quick Stop. "Ma'am, do you give cash back on a purchase?"

"No sir, we don't. But there's an ATM machine over there."

Drove to Cracker Barrel. "Ma'am, do you give cash back on a purchase?"

"No sir, I'm sorry. We don't."

Quick Stop #2. "No, sorry. You might try the Cracker Barrel."

Walgreen's Drug Store. "Yes sir, we do."

"Bingo!" Looking around, my eyes fell on a nifty pair of aviator sunglasses, the kind Ben Affleck wore in the movie *Pearl Harbor*. "I'll take these."

"That'll be $14.99, plus tax."

"Alrighty, I'll put that on my Capital One credit card, and I'd like twenty dollars cash back, please."

"Sir, we don't give cash back on credit cards, just debit cards."

"You're kidding."

"No sir. Just debit cards."

Think, O'Brien! What now? "Ma'am, I'll take this three-dollar tube of toothpaste and ten dollars back on my debit card."

"Sir, I'm sorry, but we can only give money back on purchases of five dollars or more."

"Okay, I'll take two tubes of toothpaste and ten dollars back."

Can you believe it? Insufficient funds available! I tried again. "I'll take two tubes of toothpaste and five dollars back, please." Unbelievable! Insufficient funds. "Let's try three dollars back."

"Sir, the machine won't authorize less than five dollars."

Now what? "I've *got* it! I'll buy the two tubes of toothpaste on my credit card, then immediately return the products for a cash refund." I bought the two tubes of toothpaste, walked in a seven-yard circle, and returned the toothpaste.

"Sir, we can only credit your credit card account. We can't give you cash back on returns."

"Well, how am I supposed to get through the toll roads?"

"How are you supposed to do *what*?"

"Let me speak to your manager, please."

"Mr. Martinez, would you come to the register, please? Mr. Martinez, to the register, please."

"What seems to be the problem, sir?"

"Thank you for asking, sir. I need toll money."

"You need toll money?"

"Yes sir. Look, I am holding six dollars worth of Colgate Teeth Whitening Toothpaste. I will sell these two tubes of toothpaste to you, or anyone you know, for four dollars."

"No, no, no!"

"But you'll save two dollars, and I can get through the toll booths."

"Get through *what*?"

"The toll roads. I need cash and all I have is toothpaste."

"Give him his money back."

"Hallelujah! I could kiss you!"

"*No*! Please, just go!"

One toll stop. A second. A third. Uh-oh, a fourth! $2.50! I have $2.06. "Good evening, ma'am. I've got $2.06. Do you take credit cards?"

"No, cash or checks."

"I don't have a check and only have $2.06 in cash. Will that do?"

"No, it costs $2.50."

"Look, I can't back out of this line or back down the turnpike. I've got no check, and I'm forty-four cents short. What can I do?"

"Give me your driver's license. I'll write down your number. You'll have ten days to mail in the money."

"Deal! I'll take it!"

"A little luck at last," I think as I pull away from the toll booth. "It's time to get to the hotel and put this day to bed."

Cell phone rings. Son Kris's number appears. I answer. "Hello, Dad. A pipe burst and there's water everywhere in our house!"

How hard could it be to fly from Waco, Texas, to Ocala, Florida, for my niece's wedding? Momma told me there'd be days like this!

This Ability or Disability

To become a world-class archer, you need many things: determination, equipment, practice, and positive mental tenacity. But apparently, you *don't* need two arms. Or any arms.

Leonard Loftis and Mark Stutzman, superior archers from Iowa, have one arm and no arms, respectively. Loftis lost his left arm in a motorcycle accident as a teenager. Stutzman was born without arms.

Loftis set a record at the National Field Archery Association Indoor Nationals by pulling the bowstring back with his teeth. Biting and pulling a piece of leather strap connected to the bowstring, he shot 116 bullseyes in 120 attempts! His final score of 596 of a possible 600 set a new national record.

Stutzman, positioning himself to shoot, sits in a chair, holds the bow with his right foot, and releases a shoulder-strapped mechanical trigger device with his jaw. Both archers compete in traditional competition only.

Stutzman, whose dream is to compete in the Olympics, says, "I eat, brush my teeth, and shave with my feet. If I can shoot a bow with no arms," he said, "then anybody can fulfill their dreams."

Officers and participants in national archery associations express astonishment at the ability of the two accomplished archers. Spectators initially see two men seeking to compete with disability. When the competition begins, however, whispered talk of *disability* gives way to profound respect for *this ability* of theirs.

And just like that, we're all disarmed.

Wally Christian's Twelve-foot Pole

"Welcome to Texas," Wally Christian greeted me my first week on the job.

"Thank you, Wally. Kay and I and the family are happy to be here."

"Let me give you some friendly advice now that you're a Texan."

"Please do. I'm sure I have lots to learn."

"Well, for starters, never ask a man if he's from Texas."

"Really? Why is that?"

"'Cause if he's from Texas, he'll tell you soon enough. And if he's not, there's no need embarrassing him."

"I'll remember that," I said with a laugh.

"Next, you'll find Texans are basically good people, but there *are* some scoundrels here like anywhere else."

"I'm sure that's right. Some days, I'll probably be one of 'em."

"Well, if you ever need to borrow my twelve-foot pole, just let me know."

"Twelve-foot pole? What would I do with a twelve-foot pole?"

"Oh, just a little something I invented."

"Oh, okay, but what would I need a twelve-foot pole for?"

"It's for people you wouldn't touch with a ten-foot pole."

DEATH

Buck Gibson Survives Hell

"Sharks ate between 500 and 600 of us. They ate until they were full."

Germany surrendered to the Allies in the European Theater of WWII. Yet the battle raged on in the Pacific Theater, where Japan refused to surrender. U.S. casualties at Normandy numbered nearly 7,000. An invasion of Japan promised approximately 500,000 American casualties! Enter President Truman's earth-shattering, albeit top secret decision: America would drop the world's first atomic bomb over Japan.

The *USS Indianapolis*, with its 1200-member crew, delivered the nuclear weapon, "Little Boy," to Tinian Island in the South Pacific Ocean on July 26, 1945, then sailed for naval maneuvers at Guam.

Shortly after midnight on July 30, a Japanese submarine commander ordered the firing of six torpedoes into the unsuspecting American cruiser. Two missiles exploded against "Indy," sinking her in twelve minutes. Her SOS was never received.

The survivors were battered by a savage sea, blistered by the sun, suffered from hypothermia, and endured physical and mental exhaustion, salt-sea water poisoning, hallucinatory dementia, hunger, thirst, and shark attacks.

"How long were you in the water?" I ask Buck Gibson of Mt. Calm, Texas.

"I was in the water 114 hours, almost 5 days, before they rescued us," the gunner's mate third class told me.

"How many of you survived?"

"317. They say around 900 of us went in the water. Another 300 were killed instantly, most while sleeping. So 317 of 900 survived in the water. 317 of 1200 total."

"I can't imagine."

"Sharks ate between 500 and 600 of us. They ate until they were full. Then they'd leave and come back later. We'd fight to get in the middle of the circle. They'd eat the outside ones, sometimes eating the bottom half, but the life vest would keep the torso afloat. One man had his wife's name tattooed on his arm. All that was left was his arm to identify him and notify his wife."

A survivor testifies in the book *In Harm's Way*: "The worst part was giving up my life, accepting that I was going to die—it wasn't the sharks, and it wasn't seeing your buddies die. It was when you realize you're going to die. And we were young men, healthy men. All of a sudden, there's no chance; we can't make it. They've forgotten us. We can't last forever—we're gonna die."[13]

Wife by his side, Gibson shares with me, "Men fought, even killed, to get in the middle of the circle. Stabbings happened and everything. Maybe the salt water made some mad. Several men drifted out alone, easy targets for the sharks. We watched the water turn red. Sharks ate almost 600 of us. Mornings and evenings were the worst."

"How do you ever get over something like that?"

"You never get over it. Best thing you can do is stay busy. Now that I'm retired, I probably think about it more than ever. It's probably worse now than it used to be."

"He has nightmares," Mrs. Gibson adds, "waking up screaming sometimes still today. And that was 1945."

Mercy!

I'm told that sailors share a saying as ships sail under the Golden Gate Bridge heading out to sea: "Going out to sea is the worst of hell; coming back is the best of hell."

Perhaps. But I suspect Buck Gibson relives the *worst* of hell, every night, sometimes screaming.

And survives.

---

13. Doug Stanton, *In Harm's Way* (New York: Holt & Co., 2001), 237.

Hot LZs

"Got smoke! Roger! Comin' in."

Three thousand feet high in the chopper, we Air Assault grunts see it. *Red smoke!* Hot LZ (landing zone)! Lead flying! Heart racing! Forty-four seconds to "get my house in order!" I'm scared. We all are. Can't show it. All faking it. Are we dying?

Never will I forget that moment. "Those who have seen war never stop seeing it." I see the red smoke every day. Death opens the door. Inviting us in.

Is this how it ends? In Vietnam?

One of the lucky ones am I. 58,220 other GIs are not. Another 1,601 Americans unaccounted for. 3,000,000 North and South Vietnamese annihilated. The American War, they call it. Hell, we call it.

"*Red smoke! Hot LZ!* Enemy firing! Welcoming committee!" Door gunners firing 600 rounds per minute, 10 bullets per second.

Training trains you to shoot. Doesn't train you to get shot.

"*Prepare to jump!* Hover and jump! Ready? *JUMP! Get out! Jump! Out!*"

Springing into fifty years of future nightmares, I leap.

They're gone! Enemy disappears. Ghosts! Moles! Gone!

We live!

Learning the Rest of the Story Fifty Years Later

Our platoon had been cutting trail through triple-canopy jungle in Vietnam all day, as we had for days and weeks. Exhausted from laboring in the tropical sauna and having seen no sign of enemy activity, we were hoping, "Maybe Lt. Rumcik will reduce our percentage of guard alert tonight." Fewer guards equals more sleep.

And he did.

"Only one guard per hour. You men have earned some good shut-eye."

Most of us would get a full night's sleep. No one would miss more than an hour.

Our NDP (Night Defensive Perimeter) formed a circle. If you picture the face of a clock, the trail leading into our nighttime fighting/sleeping positions was located at 6 o'clock. Each guard planted himself facing down the fresh path we had carved into the jungle. As darkness fell, we set out claymore mines, ate our c-rations, drank coffee, and then crashed for the night.

Danny Boy Davis (name changed), pulling guard between 1 and 2 a.m., committed the unpardonable sin: he fell asleep on guard duty! At the 1:00 position, Vinnie Velussi (name changed) awakened and arose to relieve himself or smoke a joint. As he looked sleepy-eyed in the direction of the trail, a blurry nightmare shocked him awake!

Doubled over sleeping Davis, knife drawn at our sentry's throat, crouched a Viet Cong soldier. The silent assassin moved to slash Davis's throat, then eased around the perimeter to slice the rest of ours. (My 7:00 position yielded me next, or last.)

Shouting, swearing, firing his M16, Velussi jolted us upright! His position-mate, Bubba Rolando, jumped up, grabbed his weapon, and gave devil-may-die chase after the fleeing guerrilla. Eyeing the back of the bolting enemy, clutching my weapon, I sprinted after Rolando. Downhill we raced to a narrow stream at the bottom of the hill. Searching left, then right, we found nothing. He vanished in the night.

My action and Rolando's, while lauded as heroic, was insanely foolish. For one, we could have tripped the wires of our own claymore mines and blown ourselves to pieces. Two, we might have been killed or wounded by a booby trap the intruder could have constructed before invading our camp. Three, we might have raced headlong into an ambush. Four, the Viet Cong might have hidden and picked us off as we ran recklessly down the trail. This impulsive action constituted my most egregious mistake in my tour of duty. I made others; all combat soldiers do. But this was the worst.

Years later, I would learn the rest of the story.

Several of us old Nam soldiers, now in our seventies, find each other on social media and commit to reunite before we "kick the bucket." Four of us—Rolando, Sizemore, Wilson, and O'Brien—rent a cabin for a weekend in the Smoky Mountains near Gatlinburg, Tennessee. We bring along our wives or girlfriends, eat steaks, consume beverages, and escort our ladies down memory lane with embellished tales of lore. The longer the night, the emptier the glass; the emptier the glass, the taller the tale.

And then comes the part of the VC chase I never knew.

"Remember the night, OB, when you and Rolando chased the Viet Cong down the hill away from the night camp, only to lose him near the stream of water below?" Sizemore, our old sniper, asks.

"Oh, gosh, yes. I was a fool for doing that. Rolando, we could've been killed! Were we crazy?"

"That, or high," he cracks.

"Why the twenty-seven NVA [North Vietnamese Army] didn't take you guys out, I'll never know," Sizemore continues.

"What are you talking about?" I ask.

"What d'ya mean, what am I talkin' about?"

"I mean, what are you talking about, twenty-seven NVA?"

"C'mon, Obie," Rolando protests. "You know what he's talking about."

"No, I don't."

"The twenty-seven NVA that had us surrounded down by the river. C'mon, Obie. I thought you were drinking Coke tonight."

"Guys, I don't have any idea what you're talking about. What d'ya mean, twenty-seven NVA?"

"Obie, I told y'all everything a coupla weeks after that, when we got back together at Camp Evans. Don't ya remember?"

"I don't remember a thing 'cause I never heard a thing."

"Maybe he's right," Rolando says, "'cause we didn't hooch together or anything."

"Okay, I'm all ears now."

"Obie, I swear to God, I thought you knew," Sizemore begins. "Me and the other three snipers from Alpha, Bravo, and Charlie companies were positioned in proximity to the stream. Lt. Rumcik knew."

"Okay, go ahead."

"We heard the gunfire, the chaos, then watched the sh*t play out through our starlight scopes. Twenty-seven NVA had you and Bubba [Rolando] surrounded. Our fingers were on fire as we watched. We woulda done all we could. But if they opened up on you, you were swiss cheese; probably woulda got us all."

"Why am I just now hearing this?"

"I dunno, I thought you knew, Obie; thought I told you."

"I thought everybody knew," Rolando adds. "Now you do."

"What are we doing here, Bubba? We should be dead!" I assert.

"No sh* t!" he says.

"The only thing I figure," Sizemore concludes, "was they had orders to make it further down south by dawn for a bigger operation; couldn't get sidetracked on you two John Waynes—not with your platoon up the hill, anyway. They didn't know about us snipers. We coulda got maybe eight or nine of 'em, maybe more. But you wouldn't've been alive to know it."

"Kay, our children were almost some other man's."

"How do you know they're not?" she says with a wink.

Drink-spewin', knee-slappin' laughter sprays the room.

Listen carefully, some say. On a still, quiet night in the Smoky Mountains of East Tennessee, you can still hear rip-roarin' laughter echoing through the canyons.

Life or Death in Vietnam

After a year of army training at Fort Bragg, North Carolina; Fort Polk, Louisiana; Fort Benning, Georgia; and Fort Polk a second time, I stepped off the plane on March 4, 1971, onto Vietnamese soil. We landed in Bien Hoa, then bused seven miles to Long Binh, America's largest military installation in Vietnam. We grunts were given a one-week last-chance crash course in combat and survival tactics, then we moved out to our assigned units.

101st Airborne Division troops awaited my arrival in Quang Tri Province below the Demilitarized Zone (DMZ), which encompassed the South and North Vietnamese borders. Within my first week with my new unit, I viewed fifty or so black body bags containing KIA American soldiers being loaded on a plane for their journey home, took sniper fire while pulling guard duty at night, and received a Dear John letter from my girlfriend back home. War is hell.

Our company soon relocated to "the boonies." One blazing hot day with temperatures high enough to melt our crayons, we were sitting around our day defensive perimeter under open skies, shirts off like we were on the beach. Some of the guys were writing letters home or rereading old ones. Others were snoozing or tanning, God only knows why. A few men were cleaning their weapons. Two or three here and there were huddled smoking and talking about girls back home.

I looked up and spotted an unsuspecting Viet Cong fighter in black pajama-like dress, pointed straw hat, and sandals, carrying an

AK-47 and leisurely strolling our way. Our eyes collided! He froze! Panicked! Turned and sprinted back in the direction he had come!

"Henson! Henson! Pieface! Grab your radio! Let's go!"

Private Pieface Henson and I pursued the enemy. "Radio Lt. Rumcik! Tell him we've got contact. In pursuit. Will communicate!"

Through the jungle we pursued the Viet Cong. Ten, fifteen minutes into the chase, we crested and descended a small hill to find ourselves staring at wide-open acres of rice paddies in lowlands leading to a distant village. Stooped men, women, and children worked hoeing rice. They froze, looking up, frightened, into the rifle barrels of two threatening American dogfaces. We counted nineteen of them. The men, dressed exactly as the Viet Cong fighter, could be his comrades. The armed enemy might be among them, incognito, AK-47 lying beneath the water. We didn't know.

"What are we going to do?" Pieface asked nervously.

"*HANDS UP!*" I screamed, motioning. "*IN THE AIR! HIGH UP!*"

Hoes dropped. Arms raised high. Faces dripped fear.

"Hand me the phone. Red Baron 5, Come in. Come in, Red Baron, 5! Red Top, here. Come in, over!"

"Red Baron 5 here. Come in, Red Top. Over."

"Got nineteen Vietnamese captured. Chopping rice. Can't tell friend or foe. Village across the way. Do you read? Over."

"Copy, Red Top, loud and clear. Your call. Take no prisoners. Do you read? Read back. Over."

"Roger. My call. Take no prisoners. Wilco. Over."

"Copy, Red Top. Out."

Now what? The call was mine. Our platoon couldn't transport nineteen prisoners with us through the jungles. We couldn't let them go; they might be Viet Cong guerrillas by night, or the Viet Cong soldier could be one of them. With our camp position known, the VC could attack us that night, or mortar us, perhaps killing some, many, most, or all of us. On the other hand, if we killed the nineteen, many, or all of them, could be mere civilians. What could we do? Their lives or ours?

This is what we did.

"Pieface, when I give the signal, start firing. We're gonna fire over their heads, in front of 'em, anywhere but at 'em, you understand? Don't you dare shoot a single one of 'em, or I'll have you court martialed, you hear me?"

"I hear ya."

"We're gonna scare 'em outta their minds; get 'em outta here. When I count to three, go crazy! Start screaming, firing. You ready?"

"Ready."

"1, 2, 3, *GO!*"

RAT-A-TAT-TAT! RAT-A-TAT-TAT-TAT! RAT-A-TAT-TAT-TAT, POP-POP-POP, POP-POP-POP-POP, POP-POP-POP-POP!

"*Didi mao! Didi mao!* [Get out of here!]"

RAT-A-TAT-TAT, RAT-A-TAT-TAT, POP-POP-POP!

The petrified Vietnamese sprinted through the rice paddies to the distant village—men, women, and children (who often served as fighters too), never stopping or looking back until they reached their homes a horizon away.

We returned to our defensive perimeter, reported to the lieutenant, and moved our camp for the night. Everyone lived.

At least for one more night.

Not Again?

Telling stories is like telling jokes. Look out! 'Cause swappin's gonna break out sure as the world. Sometimes you swap knee-slappers. Sometimes tearjerkers. Just depends. Always, though, you gotta outdo each other. You've been there.

Well, last Wednesday I told Sam Smith a story. He returned the volley before I was through laughin' at my tall tale. Outdid me, too, and this one was a tearjerker. Swore it was true. "Ask anybody in Pittsburg, Texas," he insisted.

Seems everybody in Pittsburg, Texas, knew Dub Curtis. "Dub wasn't born right," folks said. Locals there whispered, "Ol' Dub, bless his heart—ol' Dub's a chicken leg shy of a picnic."

Dub must have been fifty, maybe sixty years old. But his mind was that of a ten-year-old. Dub wore a cowboy hat, cowboy boots, and toy pistols on his hips. Every day. That was Dub's outfit. Always had been. Always would be. That was just Dub.

Mr. Edward Harris, the banker, would often play with Cowboy Dub by meeting him around town and challenging him to "slap leather." Dub would draw his toy pistol fast as he could as Mr. Harris reached for his imaginary sidearm. High drama at high noon in Cowboy Dub's Wild, Wild West World of Pittsburg, Texas.

One day the Texas Rangers came to town. An escaped convict had made his way to that neck o' the woods. The Rangers always got their man.

Two Rangers in Stetsons turned the corner of the street where Mr. Ed Harris often met Dub in their ritual showdown. There stood Dub Curtis. Dub drew first and fast. Toy pistols in each hand a'blazin'.

The Rangers riddled Dub's body with bullets. Dub slumped lifeless into the streets of Pittsburg.

Pittsburg slumped lifeless into the pits of despair. Night fell. Stars, too. Darkness stole the sun. Trees sobbed. Birds wept. Crickets muted.

Sam had me with this story.

"How does it feel to aim for a guilty man, only to realize innocent blood stains your hands?" he probes.

"Ask the Pharisees. Sadducees. Romans. Ask me. I'm asking you."

Paying the Price

On February 3, 1998, Karla Faye Tucker became the first woman executed in Texas in more than one hundred years. Found guilty of the pickax murders of Jerry Lynn Dean and Deborah Thornton, she died of lethal injection in the Texas state penitentiary in Huntsville.

On June 11, 1983, Karla, her live-in lover Danny Garrett, and several friends began a weekend binge of drug abuse. After a couple of days of shooting heroin, smoking cocaine, and popping pills, Karla and Danny broke into Jerry Lynn Dean's apartment, where Dean and his new acquaintance, Deborah Thornton, lay asleep in bed. The gruesome murder that followed repulsed the nation. The two murderers were sentenced to death.

Karla was raised in a violent home. Her father was a physically abusive alcoholic. He and Karla's mother fought constantly. Karla began smoking marijuana with her older sisters at the age of seven or eight. By age ten she was shooting heroin. By seventh grade she had dropped out of school.

When her parents divorced, Karla lived with her mother, who forced her into prostitution. Karla was fourteen. One day Karla's mother laughingly informed her that she was conceived as the result of an affair, deeply hurting, angering, and haunting Karla with the disclosure.

Karla Faye Tucker was reared in a violent world of physical abuse, alcoholism, drug abuse, and sex trafficking. Nothing about her upbringing excuses Karla's grotesque crime. There is always a story, but not all stories excuse. *"Guilty!"* cried the jury. *"Death!"* fell the sentence. Knowing Karla's story, however, may at least help us understand a little of what we probably can never fully understand.

Sometimes a little understanding makes possible a lot of forgiveness. Mary Alice and Charlie Wise became like family to Karla. For years, the Wises have led a Bible study on Tuesday nights in the Mountain View Prison Unit for women in Gatesville, Texas, where Karla was incarcerated on death row. Mary Alice and Charlie told me, "Karla is one of the most radiant Christians we have ever known. We love her and forgive her, and so does God."

Karla confessed her sins, repented, begged God for forgiveness, and received Christ as her Savior. "When I was forgiven and experienced forgiveness," she shares, "it freed me inside to soar. I went higher and deeper with the Lord."

In her book *Set Free*, Linda Storm quotes Mary Alice. "The thing that affects me most about Karla," Mary Alice says, "is the way she completely disarms people with the love of God. I have never met anyone with such an all-out love for Jesus."

Mary Alice and Charlie shared with me, "Karla is like having a chaplain 24/7 in the prison. She genuinely loves her fellow inmates and ministers to them with the love of Christ. How we wish the state would give her life without parole instead of taking her away from these women who need her so badly and follow her like sheep. She loves them and assures them God does, too."

Alas, it was not to be.

In AD 33, Christ paid the price for Karla's sins. On February 3, 1998, Karla paid the price for her crime.

"Playing Chicken" versus Eating Chicken

Given a choice between "playing chicken" or eating chicken, I prefer the latter. Evolutionary biologists, I would think, should give me a passing grade on that test. To pass along our genes to the next generation, they say, we must do three things: avoid our enemies, find something to eat, and find a mate.

Regarding playing chicken, Darrell Welch, my ninety-year-old friend, was a fighter pilot in WWII. Darrell achieved "acedom" by shooting down five of Hitler's Nazi planes. Recently, I read a story in *American Fighter Aces and Friends Bulletin* about Darrell's sky battle with German dogfighter, Wolfgang Dreifke.

"I read your story, Darrell, about your aerial showdown with Wolfgang Dreifke over Tunisia in 1943."

"Oh, you did? He ejected and survived. We wrote each other letters after the war."

"You must have nerves of steel, my friend. I can't imagine what it would be like to engage in life and death battles 10,000 feet in the air."

"Reckon I'd kinda been prepared for it growing up."

"Oh? How's that?"

"My brothers and I used to play chicken, different kinds of games of chicken all the time. Air battles are kinda like that."

"So you played chicken with Wolfgang Dreifke and won?"

"Reckon I did. We were trying to shoot each other down for sure. I was flying a P-38. He was flying a Me-109. We were both missing our shots. Finally, we just flew straight at each other. Head on. I wasn't gonna blink. Guess we were playing chicken like me and my brothers used to. At the last possible moment he chickened and turned sharp left. When he did, the whole side of his plane appeared right in front of me. I couldn't miss."

Sometime later, Darrell and I found ourselves at a church potluck supper, with "The Gospel Bird," fried chicken, stacked high on serving platters. As Darrell reached for a fried chicken leg, I couldn't resist. "Hey, my ol' fighter jock friend, you rather play chicken or eat one?"

"Depending on who cooked it"—he grinned slyly—"I could be doing both."

We laughed, which, my friends, brings us full circle: playing chicken versus eating chicken.

What do you say we avoid our enemies, find a mate, and find something to eat?

The Day the Taliban Turned Around

"Don't worry. If anyone comes searching for foreigners, we will tell them we know none. You are not like other foreigners. We will not let them harm you."

Following the terrorist attacks on America on September 11, 2001, our United States military moved forcefully into Iraq and Afghanistan, continuing to do so for nearly two decades. In those early years, terrorists and suspected terrorists were detained at the U.S. Naval Base on Guantanamo Bay, Cuba. There they were subjected to intense interrogation, perhaps torture, by the CIA and their contracted personnel. In 2005, word leaked that American interrogators had threatened to, and then did, flush the Koran down a toilet in an attempt to move prisoners to cooperate in questioning. Fact or allegation? Unknown. Muslims, however, believed the former and immediately become inflamed worldwide.

Our daughter was living in a remote Afghan village in the summer of 2005 with a team of five, teaching literacy classes to girls and tutoring women in English, which would help them advance in the workplace. Tensions were high in the village as the Taliban rioted and mobilized toward areas where Westerners lived and worked. The townspeople anticipated serious trouble for their American guests.

"They're coming! They're coming! We heard from our people in the mountains! You must hide! They're coming!"

The Taliban warriors were only a two-day journey away. "What did you do?" I asked our daughter.

"We prayed. Although it might not make sense to an outsider, all five of us and eight other Americans in the village felt peaceful about staying put."

"It's a good thing I didn't know about any of this, or I would have died!"

"Our Afghani friends hid us in an underground one-room basement for two days and two nights. Our hosts would sneak us food and give us updates they heard. 'A riot has now happened in another town. They are getting closer. They are only a half-day's journey away now. We will pray more. Pray, too. Do not worry! No one will know you are here. We will tell them *no foreigners here. You must be mistaken.*'

"As heartfelt as their words were, we all knew the power and connections of the Taliban. There was no doubt they would find us if they wanted to. We prayed several times, in some sense all the time."

"Was there no way out?" I persisted.

"The United States Embassy had an evacuation plan, and we were on standby."

"*Standby!* When do you call? When do they come!?"

"It may have been too late. But after two days and two nights in that small underground room, we received unbelievable news! 'They're headed away from our town. AWAY from our town!' We looked at our messenger in shock, then each other, stunned! 'We do not know why,' he panted. 'But they have turned and are going towards another town. Seems they will not come for you!'"

"O, Lord, I'm dying just listening to you! Your mother would have had a heart attack!"

"Amazingly, Dad, throughout this whole harrowing experience, I don't remember feeling scared."

"That's crazy!"

"I remember the sense of community built, and the relationships that deepened. I recall the peace I felt after praying. But I don't remember being scared."

"What a story!"

"I'll never forget the feeling of being valued and protected by a culture so different than my own. And I will always—*always*—remember the look of wonder on our Afghani friends' faces when they realized they had just witnessed a miracle."

Silence.

The Moral of Jimmy's Story

(Names changed)

In high school he was known throughout two or three counties, not just in his hometown. Jimmy was a great athlete, probably 6'4", maybe 6'5" and filled out. Basketball and football seemed to have been invented for the natural all-star. College was free for Jimmy. Neither grades nor girls proved a problem. Celebrity status comes with perks.

After college, Jimmy married Lou Ellen. They had a daughter and then a son. Jimmy sold insurance. Success came as easy as athletics.

Jimmy started drinking too much. In time, too much became *way* too much. Lou Ellen pleaded. Some nights Jimmy didn't come home. Some days he couldn't remember where he had been the night before. Jimmy was an alcoholic. Lou Ellen and the children paid the price. Jimmy did, too.

Young daughter Lisa would jump up in her daddy's lap as he sat in his easy chair before dinner and beg, "Daddy, please don't go away tonight. It makes Momma sad. And we all miss you." Jimmy's heart was touched. Then he would leave after dinner.

Business suffered. Creditors sent notices. People talked. "It's so sad about Jimmy. Beautiful wife and family, good business, but he's drinking it away."

Lou Ellen and the children suffered Jimmy's alcoholism for years. Then one day, Lou Ellen couldn't take it any longer. "You are going to have to choose between the bottle and me and the kids. We can't take this anymore!" Jimmy went out that night.

The divorce was no surprise in the community. "I don't know how she took it as long as she did," rang the sentiment. Lou Ellen got the house, the car, the kids, the bills. Jimmy got the gutter, as bad became worse.

Jimmy and I were longtime friends. I saw him often before he died. We talked a lot. He came to hear me preach.

Jimmy lost his family, his reputation, his job, and, finally, his life. Before his end, he had stopped drinking, joined AA, and lived alone with his regrets. When his granddaughter ran away from home, he took her in. Called his daughter and lamented, "My life has caused so much pain to so many good people. I hurt you and your mother and brother. Hell, I hurt myself. I am so sorry, honey; but I know I can't go back. Maybe at least I can do some good now. Let her stay. Please."

One night after grandfather and granddaughter had finished dinner, his sweet second chance kissed him on the cheek, said, "I love you," received her grandfather's blessing in return—"I love you, too, Sugar"—then walked down the hall to her bedroom. The loud gunshot coming from her room ended everyone's hopes.

Jimmy never really lived after that. I preached his funeral later that year.

What is the moral of the story? I don't feel like giving one.

REDEMPTION

A Hard Head and a Concrete Court

The area is rough. Police are forbidden to go into the neighborhood except in pairs, per order of the New Orleans Police Department.

Idolizing evangelist Billy Graham, and having read David Wilkerson's book *The Cross and the Switchblade*, a gripping account of the author's work with inner-city gangs, I feel inspired.

"I think I might go down into the old Irish Channel and try to do some good," I muse one evening.

"Oh? How might you do some good?" Kay asks.

"I dunno. Every night on the evening news someone else is getting robbed, or shot, or arrested for drugs."

"And just how might you help with that?"

"I dunno. I just think poverty, joblessness, drugs, no education, racial discrimination, all feed the despair and crime."

"Well, I certainly agree with that, but how are you gonna help?"

"I dunno. I was thinking for one, I could show them someone cares about them. And maybe lead some to trust God with their lives and turn things around."

"Okay, and how are you gonna do that?"

"David Wilkerson took his Bible into gang-infested ghettos and asked gang members to put their hope in Christ instead of crime."

"Oh? And what happened?"

"They did it."

"They did it? Just like that? Maybe so, but stories like that are usually much bigger than that. You know how violent that area is.

I'm not sure a White preacher in a depressed all-Black area that police can't even enter except in pairs is a good idea. Maybe Black ministers would be more welcome and effective."

"Don't worry. I got this."

Taking my Bible with me, I drive to the old Irish Channel the next afternoon. Standing on the street corner on 3701 Annunciation Street a block off the New Orleans riverfront, I "preach" to the best of my limited ability. Sharing the gospel with passersby, intending to save souls, I give it all I have.

I'm not sure how Billy Graham and David Wilkerson do it, but the only thing I "save" is further humiliation by leaving when I do.

After getting mocked mercilessly, laughed out of the neighborhood, I mope over the next several days. My hard head is ripe for Kay's wisdom.

"What's wrong?"

"Nothing."

"Wanna tell me about it?"

"No, nothing's wrong."

"You sure act like something's wrong."

"Well, it's not."

In a little while as I sit disheartened on the couch, Kay tries again. "Honey, what's wrong? Does it have anything to do with going down into the rough part of town?"

"I don't wanna talk about it."

When there is no change in the demeanor of "Mr. Sunshine," Kay returns, puts my basketball in my lap, and sets my tennis shoes on the floor in front of me. Saying nothing, she turns and walks away. "What's this?" I grumble.

"Oh, I don't know; think about it."

"I don't wanna think about it."

"You don't have to."

I'm slower than a week in jail, but after a while it hits me! "Perfect! Next time I'll go back with my basketball, not my Bible. Connection before direction. Player before pray-er. Water to wine, one time; playground to holy ground this time."

Once, the Voice boomed, "Moses, take off your shoes!" I hear, "Randall, put on your shoes!"

Kay's a genius.

If, however, you think I was mercilessly hooted out of the neighborhood for carrying a Bible, you should've seen how brutal it was when the skinny White boy with the chicken legs returned with a basketball.

Until the games started.

God loves this stuff.

God must have elbowed Gabriel, winked, and said, "Watch this." Every pass I make is perfect; every shot I take kisses the net. Every play brings hoots and high-fives on the sidelines. In these serious pick-up games, losers get off the concrete court; winners stay on. Those are the rules.

Do miracles never cease? The only White boy on that inner-city playground stays on the court 'til dark. God has fun. So do I.

And a ministry is born.

A Killer Gets Life

On December 20, 1974, ten-year-old Chris Carrier of Coral Gables, Florida, stepped off the school bus in front of his house for the Christmas holidays only to disappear into the clutches of evil. Just like that, Chris was gone.

December 21, 22, 23, Christmas Eve. No Chris. Christmas Day dawns. Christmas dies. No Chris. Who abducted Chris? And why? Where is he? Is he alive? Or dead? Will he ever be seen again?

Then the news! December 26, a hunter finds a bloody boy deep in the Florida Everglades. Stabbed with an ice pick, burned with cigarettes, and shot in the temple, the child had been left for dead. It was Chris.

Chris was alive. The bullet had entered one temple and exited the other. Bloodied and blinded in one eye, miraculously Chris survived the elements, including wild animals, in a state of unconsciousness for six days.

Authorities immediately identified a fifty-five-year-old ex-convict, David McAllister, as the prime suspect in the case. McAllister had been fired from his job of caring for Chris's elderly uncle. No direct evidence, however, connected McAllister to the crime. The case was never prosecuted.

More than two decades later, Coral Gables police major, Charles Scherer, originally frustrated by the case, learned that McAllister, now seventy-seven, was confined to a Miami nursing home. The detective made a house call. Then again. And again. "He fits the composite to a

T," detective Scherer told the Associated Press. "I was sure of it then, and I'm sure of it now."[14]

After several interviews, McAllister confessed to the kidnapping, though not the shooting. Since the statute of limitations had expired, the guilty man could not be charged. Norma Carrier, Chris's mother, also convinced of McAllister's guilt from the beginning, admitted, "Forgiveness is very, very hard, but I'm glad that it's finished."

Chris is by now a thirty-two-year-old husband and father of two young daughters, Amanda, age two, and Melodee, seven months old. Chris's blind left eye barely opens. Recently, he has graduated from the Southwestern Baptist Theological Seminary in Fort Worth, Texas. While serving as a minister to youth, Chris learns of McAllister's confession.

Chris begins visiting McAllister. Over the next six days, he visits McAllister five times, taking his young daughters with him. They read the Bible during visits and pray. "Nobody would imagine that I would one day shake the hand of the man who tried to kill me," Chris relates. "But when I look at him, I don't stare at my abductor and potential murderer. I see a man very old, very alone, and scared. He's never been able to live without memories and pain. He has paid his price, served his time. I forgive him."

He says to the man who tried to kill him, "Mr. Allister, I forgive you for what happened a long time ago. I am glad we are friends now. But I want us to be friends forever. Would you like God to forgive you so we can be friends forever in Heaven?"

"Yes," McAllister whispers.

As the kidnapper and kidnapped pray together, David McAllister asks and receives God's forgiveness, asking Christ into his heart. An attempted murderer gets life.

In three weeks, McAllister is dead, resting in peace.

14. "San Marcos teacher learned to forgive through his own trauma," *Baptist Standard*, November 26, 2001, 1, 9.

All's Well That Ends Well

"Could I have a moment with you?"

"Sure. Happy to visit. How can I help?"

"Could we maybe walk over there in the corner so we can have some privacy?"

I am in Jackson, Mississippi, leading a conference for area ministers. We take a fifteen-minute mid-morning break for refreshments and conversation, and my new friend and I amble over to a corner of the room. He introduces himself and begins.

"Thank you for coming today. Long way from Texas. Welcome home."

"The pleasure of being with you saints here in Mississippi is all mine."

"I vacillated about coming today, had so much I needed to do; but in the end I knew I had to come. Had to talk to you."

"Well, I'm glad you did. How can I help? What d'ya have on your mind?"

"It's about the Mississippi College presidency."

"Oh, okay. What about it?"

"You probably know, but you were our choice of the Metropolitan Baptist Association."

"I heard that, and I'm honored."

"I'm also an alum. Did you know you had the endorsement of the MC Alumni Association?"

"I heard that, too. I'm humbled."

"I don't know for a fact, but I heard the faculty senate also endorsed your candidacy."

"The senate chair communicated that to me. Means a lot."

"Seems like everyone wanted our favorite son to come home."

"That means so much to me. Guess it just wasn't meant to be."

"That's why I came today. I have to tell you what happened."

"Oh, okay."

"We have a deacon in our church, a successful businessman, who is a trustee of the college. He was a member of the presidential search committee."

"Okay."

"I had visited with him early on to let him know the hopes of the Metro Baptist Association ministers. Then when you were not selected to be our next president, we were so disappointed."

"Thank you. So were Kay and I."

"That's why I came. I thought you deserved to know what happened."

"Well, you certainly have my attention."

"One Sunday after church I mentioned to our trustee search committee member how disappointed I was to learn you had not been selected to be the next MC president. Do you know what he said?"

"No, I don't."

"He said, 'Pastor, you're not the only one disappointed when Dr. O'Brien withdrew his name from consideration."

"*What*?"

"You didn't, did you?"

"No!"

"I know you didn't. I spoke with your friend, Emerson Beecher [name changed]. He was shocked! Said you and Kay were disappointed; that you certainly had *not* withdrawn your name from consideration."

"He's right. I did not. In fact, we were stunned. After interviews with the three of us finalists, I felt great. Everything seemed to go magically. Even the Executive Search Firm representative rushed after me as I was leaving, excitedly promising, 'You'll definitely be hearing from this committee!'"

"Well, I don't know what you do with this information, probably nothing, but I thought you, at least, deserved to know what had happened."

"Hon, guess what I learned in Mississippi," I announce to Kay upon returning home to Texas.

"That you missed me?"

"Yes, that, too."

"Okay, I give. What else? Welcome home!"

"I learned what happened with the Mississippi College presidency."

"What d'ya mean?"

"I mean the search committee was told I had withdrawn my name from consideration."

"*What*?"

"So I guess when Dr. Johnson [name changed] swore I'd come back to MC over his dead body after we decided to stay at Baylor a few years ago rather than accept that other MC position, he meant it. Or someone certainly did."

"Well, you remember what Joseph said to his brothers after they sold him into slavery, don't you?"

"Sure do. 'You meant it for evil, but God meant it for good.'"

"Well, hon, different Joseph, same God, same truth, right? We'll be just fine."

Three years later, I am named provost, then provost and executive vice president of Baylor University.

Three more years later, I am named president of Carson-Newman University.

Ten years later, I retire following a deeply meaningful, gratefully fulfilling, providentially blessed, lifetime ministry of service. "God meant it for good." For all.

(President Lee Royce, not I, was elected president of MC in 2002 and served Mississippi College sixteen record-setting years before retiring in

2018. By any standard of measurement, my friend and colleague President Royce proved one of the most successful presidents in the 192-year history of the college.)

Fishin' for Men

Can't say I ever had a barber like Bobby Clark. In fact, I can't say I ever *knew* anybody like Bobby Clark. The man could some kinda evermore fish!

Now, I'm not talkin' 'bout pond fishin', river fishin', trout fishin', deep sea fishin', or any other kind of fishin' like that. Bobby would get off from work at the end of the day, go home, get a bite to eat, pray, get in his car, and drive off. "Lord, direct me to the bar and the man you want me to witness to tonight."

With purpose in his heart and prayer on his tongue, off Bobby Clark would drive. One night it would be this beer joint, the next night another one.

This particular night, Bobby felt strongly led in answer to his prayers. He pulled into the parking lot, slid out of his car, and strolled into the dark, smoke-filled bar. Bobby's custom was to order a Coke, spy the person he believed God had brought him there to visit, then walk over and begin his ministry. Bobby saw his man.

Far in the back recesses of the room sat a depressed man, all alone, several drinks in front of him, not a few empty rounds, and a faraway look in his eye. He appeared well on his way to getting sloshed. Bobby walked over to him and asked, "May I join you?"

"Sure, why not?"

As the two talked into the evening, this is the story my barber heard:

"My wife and I had one child. Apple of our eye. Perfect family, guess you could say. One day my wife is off shopping. Ashley and I are outside playing. Sandbox. Swingset. The phone rings. I go inside to answer it. Come back out, Ashley's gone. Just a toddler. Couldn't be far. Look everywhere. Nothing! 'Ashley, where are you?' Nothing! 'Ashley, where are you?' Nothing. My heart drops. 'Ashley! Ashley!' Running here and there, I race to the neighbor's. In their backyard I see her. Bottom of their swimming pool. Lifeless. Drowned. Gone. Forever. My Ashley. Dead.

"My wife has never forgiven me. Blames me. Says it's all my fault. Finally left me. Filed for divorce. Left me all alone in my guilt. My shame. Unforgiven, unloved, despised, rejected. When she divorced me, the church declared the pulpit vacant. Said the bylaws didn't allow a divorced man to pastor the church. Now I've got nothing left, nothing at all but my pain. Nothing to live for. Nothing. Nothing at all. Nothing, nothing, nothing!"

Trying hard to escape his chamber of horrors, frantically swimming farther and farther into a luring sea of alcohol, soul tiring, spirits sinking, how long can the poor mortal survive? Is this how it all ends?

God sent a barber fishin'. Bobby Clark went fishin'. And he caught a big one!

Today, a minister is ministering again, himself fishin' for men. All because a barber named Bobby Clark got off work one day and went fishin'.

The Rain of a King

"So, you're from McComb, Mississippi?"

"Yes, I am. Why? Are you?"

"Well, I used to live there."

"Really?"

"Long time ago. Your story about McComb brought back memories. Can we talk?"

"Sure. Let me bid the parishioners a good day, then we can get comfortable on a pew and visit."

As guest minister of the day for South Main Baptist Church in Houston, Texas, I offered a sermon with an illustration about growing up in my hometown. Joining us for worship was the elderly husband of a woman undergoing cancer treatment in nearby M. D. Anderson Hospital. As we sat to visit, he began, "Thank you for making time for me. I sure appreciate it."

"The joy is mine. Tell me about you and McComb."

"Well, unlike you, I wasn't born there; but I lived there several years back in the '60s."

"You sure picked some tough years to live in McComb!"

"Tell me about it! That's what I want to talk to you about."

"Sure. I've got all the time in the world."

"Look, I've never told anyone this before."

"Well, you don't have to."

"No, really, I want to. Need to. Lived with it all my adult life. Parts I need to forgive; parts I need to forget."

"Honored to listen."

"Thanks. Guess I need a priest, a confessor maybe. Don't know if it's coincidence or providence that I'm here today."

"Well, either way, until you can do better, I'm pleased to serve. Why don't you feel free to keep your name and all others between you and God?"

"Thank you. I served a church in McComb in the '60s as one of the ministers on staff. I won't name the church or denomination."

"That's fine."

"Do you remember Freedom Summer of '64?"

"How could I forget?"

"Then you remember all the bombings of Black churches and homes of civil rights workers and sympathizers."

"Yes, I do."

"I was having an affair with a woman in the choir."

"Oh, okay."

"Her husband was a Klansman."

"Oh, my."

"The Klan was doing all the bombing."

"Yeah, I know."

"They hated Dr. King. Called him Martin Luther Coon."

"I remember."

"One night she and I were together, and she swore me to a secret. Made me swear."

"Well, you don't have to tell me."

"No, I do! Most everybody is dead now; my wife's cancer may be terminal, and who knows how much time I have left. Besides, keeping the secret was imperative so her husband and the rest of the Klan wouldn't know their plan had been leaked. If they found out she told me, they could've maybe caught on to the affair. Probably would've beat her either way, maybe killed me. Who knows? I admit I was frightened to be in possession of my newfound information."

"Good gracious! Sounds bad! I understand your affair had to remain clandestine, but the secret your paramour shared with you must have been monstrous."

"It was. Dr. King was flying to Mississippi in July for a publicized five-day visit of Greenwood, Jackson, Meridian, and Vicksburg. This was '64. Two unannounced stops would include Philadelphia and McComb. You know what had happened in Philadelphia, and McComb had bombs going off seemed like every night."

"Remember it well."

"I think Dr. King's camp thought it was too dangerous for an announced trip to McComb. He was scheduled to speak in Jackson one night, then drive down to McComb afterwards, spend the night, and meet privately with civil rights leaders the next morning."

"The Klan knew all that?"

"Yes, they did. Don't ask me how. I don't know."

"Okay."

"They were going to kill him."

"What!"

"He would be staying in the Holiday Inn. They had his room number on the balcony. An assassin lay in the bushes behind the Exxon Service Station with a clear view of Dr. King's room, waiting for him to arrive. Armed with a high-powered rifle, the assassin waited all night."

"What happened?"

"Dr. King never came."

"Thank God! But why? Do you know?"

"Rain and thunderstorms covered Jackson that night. Dr. King and his people decided to spend the night in Jackson rather than drive down to McComb in the rain. The next afternoon, they headed on to Vicksburg."

"I thought I had heard it all and read it all! This is insane!"

"Yes, it is. Four years later he was shot and killed in Memphis."

"Yes, my goodness! But he would've died four years earlier, in McComb in '64, rather than Memphis in '68, right? Right. Unbelievable!"

"I've never told anyone the story 'til now. Never told my wife about the affair, and I've never told her, or anyone else, about the Klan's plot to kill Dr. King in McComb. Thanks for letting me get all this off my chest. I think I can go back to the hospital now."

My anonymous source shared his secret with me eighteen years ago. He had waited thirty-eight years before opening his closed book. Fifty-six years have now passed since the alleged event. Many, perhaps most, maybe all of the principals are now deceased. Regardless, all names are withheld.

True story? How could one possibly say for sure? I can make no claims of veracity for the events shared with me. However, records do reveal that Dr. King traveled to Mississippi July 21, 1964, during Freedom Summer, the civil rights movement's major initiative in the state referred to as "America's dungeon." Dr. King visited Greenwood, Jackson, Meridian, Philadelphia, and Vicksburg, July 21–24, but not McComb. Moreover, Dr. King's organization was in possession of information before his departure from Montgomery for Meridian that a "guerilla group" planned to kill the high profile civil rights leader during his Mississippi visit.[15] *The Reverend, nevertheless, insisted on visiting the state. On the night of July 22, the renowned minister delivered a speech in Jackson. The* Clarion-Ledger *in Jackson reported "showers and thundershowers" for Wednesday, July 22, the night of Reverend King's planned but unannounced drive to McComb.*[16]

Dr. Martin Luther King, Jr., was shot and killed on the balcony of the Lorraine Motel in Memphis, Tennessee, April 4, 1968.

---

15. See *The Autobiography of Martin Luther King, Jr.*, ed. Clayborne Carson (New York: Warner, 2001), 250.

16. *Clarion-Ledger*, July 22, 1964, 2.

SURPRISE

A Snake Named Jake

I hate spiders and snakes. Always have. Came by it honestly. Momma hates spiders and snakes. Daddy hates spiders and snakes. All my kin hate 'em.

Northerners dislike things. Southerners *hate* 'em! If I lived in Vermont I would dislike reptiles. I live in Texas. I hate snakes. "Only good snake is a dead snake." How many times have I heard that? Said that?

Until Tuesday, June 10, 1997, I had never seen a snake that wasn't about to be dead. "Ain't no child o' mine fool enough to like no snake!" Momma always said. Snakes: fight, flight, or faint. Momma's fear never let her choose. Poor Momma. Always faintin'. Except once. Still remember it well . . .

One hot summer day at 910 Bendat Street in McComb, Mississippi, I was lying on my back in our front yard restin'. Reckon I must've been seven or eight years old. A man that old needs his rest. Slithering towards me from behind, insensitive to my geriatric needs, was what we called a king-sized rattlesnake. To be distinguished, I suppose, from a queen-sized one or a pint-sized one. Anyway, Satan sent the big one. God sent Momma.

With Leviathan less than three feet from my head, Momma comes outta nowhere, hollerin', screamin', hoe raised high overhead, attackin', "I'll kill you! I'll kill you!" I can't speak for Señor Serpent, but I thought Momma was takin' me to see Jesus. Momma's hoe fell with lightnin' fury! Again and again and again the blade slammed into its target. One little, two little, three little pieces; four little, five little . . .

After foulin' my undies and doing my whites, I vowed to become a snake killer just like Momma. Which brings me back to Tuesday, June 10, 1997.

Known in our wooded neighborhood as Randall the Reptile Eradicator, I wouldn't have believed what was to come. After all, hadn't three slimy, slithering serpents slithered into our backyard, and hadn't all three gone to meet their Maker? One by 12-gauge Remington 1100 Automatic Shotgun, one by 12.5 horse-powered 6-speed Transmatic, Transaxle, Montgomery Ward Riding Lawnmower, and one by Exxon Regular Unleaded 87 Octane gasoline with an assist from one Ohio Blue Tip Damp-proof Strike-on-the-Box, Made in the USA kitchen match? Wasn't it my call to settle the score of that Adam and Eve snake story?

So who could've guessed what was coming? As I arrived home from work and pulled into the end of our driveway, my big eyes saw it! Christopher, our eight-year-old son, and Colt, his one-year-old gray Heinz 57 cat, had cornered a foot-and-a-half-long green garden snake. Do I need to tell you my instincts?

As I came runnin' out of the garage with my Ace Hardware $24.95 garden hoe raised high overhead, Kris screamed, "*No*, Daddy, no! Don't kill him! Don't kill him! He's not hurtin' anything. He's mine and Colt's!"

"Outta the way, boy. This is a job for a man."

"Daddy, don't kill him. Please. I wanna keep him for a pet."

"A *what*? Are you crazy, son? That's a snake. If he bit you, he'd kill you!"

"Daddy, he's just a baby garden snake. We learned about them in school."

"Son, dads know a thing or two, too. He might be a garden snake today, but tomorrow he could morph into a rattlesnake or a water moccasin!"

"Daddy, please! Please let me keep him for a pet! Please, Daddy, please!"

May I interject some history at this point? My grandfather, Jesse O'Brien, had only one son to carry on the family name, although he had two wonderful daughters. His only son, Donald, my dad, had only one son, though he too has two precious daughters. For the third generation now, yours truly has two angel daughters but only one son to carry on the family name. Furthermore, Christopher came to his old man father late, a delight to his forty-year-old father's eyes. I reckon the boy is "my beloved son, with whom I am well pleased."

They don't make Ace Hardware $24.95 garden hoes like they used to. There was a time when that wooden-handled, iron-edged farm implement would've slammed itself repeatedly into that mass of danger coiled before my beady eyes. Instead, the hoe just turned, went back into our garage, and rested itself in the corner.

Today, along with our blind, deaf, eleven-year-old cocker spaniel named Katie Belle and two pampered cats named Patch and Lilia (Colt disappeared), we have an additional family member.

In Christopher's room, pampered in a cozy glass aquarium filled with leaves, sticks, crickets, and a little boy's love, lives a beautiful foot-and-a-half-long green garden snake named Jake.

Guess you could say, "Greater love hath no man than he that lay down his hoe for his son."

The Amazing Grace of Dr. Oseola McCarty

Oseola McCarty wanted to become a nurse.

Eight-year-old Oseola labored after school with her mother, grandmother, and aunt cleaning clothes in the early 1900s in Southern Mississippi. With the illness of her aunt, twelve-year-old Oseola dropped out of school to help her mother and grandmother full-time. Later, she would nurse all three of her beloved family members until their deaths.

For more than seventy years, Oseola worked as a washerwoman, never marrying. Weekly she walked to the bank to deposit what little she had left over after paying her bills and buying necessities. At the age of eighty-seven—she lived to be ninety-one, passing away in 1999—Oseola established a trust leaving *$150,000* to the University of Southern Mississippi for scholarships for needy students. "Grownups can do for themselves," she said. "I wanted to give this gift to the children."

Word travels. Oprah Winfrey hosted Oseola on her television show. So did David Letterman. Barbara Walters named Miss McCarty one of the "Top Ten Fascinating People of 1995." Featured segments about her life appeared on NPR, ABC, CBS, NBC, and BBC. President Bill Clinton wrote Miss McCarty a personal letter, then awarded her the Presidential Citizens Medal.

"I think the way we live matters, not just for now but for always," Miss McCarty said. "There is an eternal side to everything you do."

Inspired by Miss McCarty's example, Atlanta media mogul Ted Turner gave a billion dollars to the United Nations for underprivileged children. "I admire Oseola McCarty," Turner said after meeting the diminutive saint. "She gave away her entire life savings. She did more than I did. I just gave away one third—I've still got two billion left. She's the one who really deserves the credit." The aged angel protested, "People have given more than I have already."

She who had always wanted to be a nurse in order to take care of others found another way to help people in need. In amazed appreciation, Memphis's Baptist Memorial Hospital named Miss McCarty an honorary nurse. Harvard University awarded her an honorary doctorate. Doctor Oseola McCarty!

Providence is smiling. The little saint who had wanted to become a nurse became a doctor. And a lot of people in need are being taken care of.

(Adapted from Nancy Dorman-Hickson, "The Amazing Grace of Miss McCarty," *Southern Living*, February 1998)

Angels' Wings Spotted

Angels' wings are difficult to spot. Angels tend to move around incognito. Humility and service provide excellent social camouflage.

Numerous stories of heavenly visitors being entertained by unaware hosts and hostesses appear in the Good Book. The celestial beings almost always look like human beings. Recognition comes late, if at all, after which the visitor disappears.

In May 2018, the university where Kay and I served completed the winter semester. Heading into final exams, the school routinely set aside "Dead Days," where classes did not meet and students could relax a bit, exercise for stress release, enjoy comfort food in the cafeteria, and study for final exams.

Kay sat visiting with a group of young women students in the cafeteria. She asked, "Who, in your time here at the university, has been your encourager, a genuine blessing in your life, someone who truly cares about you?"

"Cookie!" three of the girls answered at once.

"Cookie? Who's Cookie? Tell me about her."

"We don't really know Cookie's real name. But she knows ours. We all call her Cookie because she bakes homemade cookies for us."

"Really? How do you know her? Is she on staff here? Where does she work?"

"Right here! She works in the cafeteria. She punches our meal ticket."

"And she makes you cookies and brings them to work?"

"Yes, and they are so yum!"

"And she knows all your names?"

"Sure does. Sweetest person ever!"

That evening Kay shared the conversation with me. "Isn't that the sweetest thing?"

"Yes, it is," I agreed. "Let me look into this. Try to find out a little more."

We learned that Cookie lived alone in a modest house nearby. She never married. Didn't drive. Walked to and from work and to the store. I mentioned to several people what I'd heard about Cookie. "This is what I'm told. Sound right to you?"

"Oh, that's Cookie alright. She's the sweetest, most giving person in the world. And she just loves these girls."

"Apparently she does. They sure love her back."

In our fall back-to-school faculty/staff meeting in August, a newly created Angel Award was being introduced by the president. The criteria for selection were read. A large crystal angel rested on the podium, along with a check to be presented. A relatively anonymous, diminutive, elderly woman sat unsuspecting in the back.

"The recipient of the Inaugural Angel Award goes to Luanna 'Cookie' Dickinson. Miss Dickinson, would you please come forward? I believe your angel wings have been spotted."

A standing ovation swept Miss Dickinson down the aisle. Tears flowing, she received the crystal angel, a monetary award, and a hug from the president. Back at work later that day, she cried again while sharing her feelings with her supervisor.

"I've been feeling so bad lately. This morning it was so hard to get out of bed. I was just hurting all over. I almost called in sick. I didn't even know anybody knew my name," she wept. "Nothing like this has ever happened to me. I didn't know when I got up today this was going to be the greatest day of my life!"

In three weeks, those sweet angel wings carried "Cookie" home.

Dining on Musgoes

Men in my family of origin are known to eat just about anything. From the mouth of my Pa, I first heard the boast, "I'll eat anything that doesn't eat me first!" Pa's son, my dad, loved a juicy piece of meat, but could eat his weight in raw oysters and crayfish claws. No comment on what he washed 'em down with. Any child in our family who balked at supper received a dish of salty words.

"Eat what's put before you, son!"

"But, Dad, it moved!"

"Fork it! Clean out your plate, boy!"

So when Miz Olivia Welch invited Kay and me to her home for musgoes after church one Sunday night, I didn't hesitate. Miz Olivia, a big-hearted widow, mother, and grandmother of several, had a much-deserved reputation in the community as one of the best cooks within many miles of the Mississippi-Louisiana state line.

"She can make a butterbean melt on your tongue!" Donald Chase declared. "And boiled okra slide down your throat before you can taste it."

Kay and I had no idea what a musgo was; but I figured if it wasn't a chitlin I'd eat it. Pig intestines? No way! Never been that hungry!

Driving over, I asked, "Hon, what d'ya think musgoes are?"

"I thought you knew. I don't know. You sure acted like you love 'em."

"What am I supposed to say, 'what's musgoes?' Anyway, we'll find out soon enough, won't we?"

***

"Hello, Miz Olivia, thanks for having us over."

"Oh, Brother O'Brien, you are always welcome in my home. I hope you like musgoes."

"Like my Pa used to say, 'I'll eat anything that don't eat me first.'"

"Well, we'll see about that."

"Miz Olivia, I gotta confess something to you."

"What is it, hon?"

"Miz Olivia, Kay and I have no idea what musgoes are."

"Oh, honey, you've never eaten musgoes? I bet you've eaten 'em your whole life; just didn't know is all."

"I dunno. Maybe so. But I don't think so. What are musgoes?"

"Honey, musgoes are everything in the refrigerator that must go."

Have I Got a Sweater For YOU

Rikki and Sean McEvay of Knoxville, Tennessee, came across some great luck, just as you are about to do. The story?

One fine day in June 2014, the McEvays' leisurely motored across the mountains to Asheville, North Carolina, for dinner. With time to kill, they decided to browse through a Goodwill store. The couple enjoyed vintage clothes and also reselling them online.

Sean's eyes fell upon an old sweater. It was black with WEST POINT written in gold letters across the front. "I thought it was pretty cool. Thought maybe it was an old basketball warm-up or something." The garment was clearly old, perhaps 1940s or '50s, Sean surmised. Other than a couple of small moth holes, it appeared in great shape. Sean decided to buy it.

"How much is this sweater?"

"I'll have to weigh it. We sell clothes by the pound."

"Okay, thank you."

"That'll be 58 cents."

"I'll take it."

Sean noticed later the word "Lombardi" written in black ink on a swatch of cloth inside the garment, but no bells or sirens went off. Upon arriving back home, he put the purchase up and forgot about it. Six months later he was watching an ESPN documentary on the life of legendary Vince Lombardi when he noticed the Hall of Famer sporting a West Point sweater exactly like Sean's 58-cent treasure.

Could it be?

The lucky couple examined the name, hired a firm to authenticate the age of the material, handwriting, and zipper, and investigated its journey to Goodwill. It turned out that Anna Wannamaker, whose late husband Bill coached with Lombardi at West Point, had donated the cardigan.

"I considered giving it to the NFL Hall of Fame," Sean shared. "Then I thought about presenting it to Vince, Jr. Rikki preferred to sell it. So we did."

Auctioned in New York City, the sweater sold for $43,020!

Which brings me to *your* good luck.

In February 2019, the United States Military Academy at West Point, New York, invited me to deliver the National Prayer Breakfast Address. I was, of course, honored to accept. A day quickly turned into a weeklong invitation, where I was privileged to speak on eight separate occasions. The joy was all mine!

On my last day, my gracious hosts presented me a striking Army sweater, black, trimmed in gray, with a large gold "A" seizing the eye. I love my sweater! Truly love it! However, recalling the McEvays' rare find, and thinking only of you, I could—perhaps, maybe, possibly—be talked into auctioning my historic West Point souvenir.

What d'ya think? "Not as famous as Lombardi," you say? Oh, sure, I agree. So we could, I suppose, meet in the middle, in good will. What d'ya say? $20,000 for a sweater, anyone?

Oh, Chute! Am I Jumping out of a Perfectly Good Airplane?

"President O'Brien, we have a really big soccer game on campus Saturday. Both teams are undefeated."

Carson-Newman University's men's soccer team was one of the best in the nation in 2013, ending the season playing for the National Championship. "Yes, I know," I said. "Kay and I wish we could be here to cheer you on, but we will be in Colorado. Our football team is playing Saturday between our son's and daughter's towns. So we decided to fly out to Colorado for the game and see our grown children as well."

"I completely understand," Assistant Coach Francois replied. "It seems like everyone will be out of town."

"Really? Everybody?"

"Our football team, our women's soccer team, our golf teams, tennis teams, and cross-country teams will all be on the road. We're afraid we won't have many people at the game."

"I see what you mean."

"I have an idea."

"What is it?"

"If we get 500 people at the game, will you jump out of an airplane?"

"Will I *what*?!"

"Yes sir, we could advertise it. If 500 people come to the game, President O'Brien will jump out of an airplane!"

"I have a better idea."

"You do? What is it?"

"*You* jump out of the airplane!"

"No sir. It has to be you, or people won't come."

"Tell you what. Make it 1,000 people and I'll do it."

"You will?"

"Yeah, 500 sounds Mickey Mouse. Small time. Go big!"

"Then you'll do it?"

"Then I'll do it."

As Kay and I watched the football game in Colorado, I kept checking the gate numbers of the soccer game back home via my cell phone. As attendance exceeded 500 before game time, I remarked, "Sure glad I agreed to 1,000 rather than 500." As attendance reached 800, I conceded, "It's over."

"Did they do it?"

"No, not yet, but they will. They're at 800 now. They'll count dogs, cats, fleas, babies, pregnancies; I'm done."

Attendance exceeded 1,000!

Both men's and women's soccer teams and coaches turned out at the East Tennessee skydiving site. Kay was on hand to collect my life insurance. People were giving high fives; it was a party atmosphere. Up, up, and away we soared into the clear blue sky in the small plane.

"Oh, chute! What am I doing?" We ascended two miles in the air. Then higher. Adrenaline, seratonin, dopamine surged through my veins.

Skydivers plunge to earth at 120 miles per hour! What am I doing?

We jumped!

I tandem jumped with an experienced instructor. We fell 1,000 feet in 10 seconds after we leaped, then fell 1,000 feet every 5 seconds at terminal velocity. I hate that word "terminal"! In less than 60 seconds we opened our chute at 5,000 feet. Silence. Total calm. We floated quietly, blissfully, toward the landing zone at a sleepy pace of 17 miles per hour. We landed. I *survived*!

"How was it? Did you like it? Was it fun? What was it like?

The questions came fast and happy.

"It was a blast!"

"Would you do it again? How does it feel? What did you learn?"

"I learned next time to change 500 attendees to 5,000."

A Sputnik and a Surprise

On October 4, 1957, the Soviet Union launched into orbit a satellite named *Sputnik*. The small, round 184-pound satellite, the world's first man-made object to circle the planet, created an immediate international uproar. Despite U.S. President Dwight Eisenhower's best attempts to assure the nation of the innocuousness of the event, America plunged headlong into a state of high anxiety.

Seared deeply within our American psyche smoldered unforgettable nightmarish scenes of Pearl Harbor. Was another surprise attack possible, even imminent? A nation that could launch a satellite into outer space could conceivably propel an intercontinental missile armed with a nuclear warhead into our country.

I was a boy of eight in 1957. How well I remember *Sputnik!* Dad named our family dog Sputnik. How could I forget?

As the Cold War developed into a mad space race and arms race between the U.S. and the U.S.S.R., who could possibly forget Soviet Premier Nikita Kruschev angrily pounding his shoe on the table at the United Nations and shouting at our U.S. Ambassador, "We will bury you!"

The Soviets, or Russians, as the terms were incorrectly used interchangeably, were our enemies. The U.S.S.R. was what President Ronald Reagan thirty years later would call "The Evil Empire."

I must say I never imagined setting foot inside Russia. Ever.

But I did.

From May 15 to 29, 2009, Kay and I and our twenty-one-year-old son Kris spent two weeks in Russia. We were there as guests of the St. Petersburg Evangelical Theological Academy, where I was invited to teach biblical studies to Russian ministers and other devout Christians who, in turn, would minister to their Russian neighbors. Academy President Sergei Nikolai and his faculty, staff, and students amazed us with their bold commitment to Christian ministry in Russian churches, homes, and addiction centers.

On Sundays we worshiped with Christian sisters and brothers in the Temple of the Gospel Evangelical Church. Hymn singing rocked the building! Pastor Nikolai invited me to preach, which I eagerly did. Many people made public decisions to follow Jesus Christ as Lord and Savior. The singing, praying, praising worship service astounded us.

Kay led two women's conferences at the church. She was embraced, hugged, and kissed by the sisters in the church. They begged her to return. Pastor Nikolai served as Bishop of 150 evangelistic churches in the St. Petersburg area alone. Revival is real.

In downtown St. Petersburg, the magnificent Russian Orthodox Kazansky Cathedral stands with its massive Greek columns anchoring the edifice's large semicircle face that fronts the busy street. There for all to see in four-foot-high red letters, spread across the top of the columns, spells "C-H-R-I-S-T-O-S V-O-S-K-R-E-S"—"Christ is Risen!"

True, America and Russia remain enemies. Also, atheism remains Russia's official state stance on religion. But in our two-week visit, we thought little of *Sputnik*, which means "fellow traveler." Instead, we celebrated our brotherhood and sisterhood with our Russian "fellow travelers" in Christ.

Truly, God's other name is *"SURPRISE!"*

Tennis, Anyone?

I'm preaching a sermon in DeGray Baptist Church in Arkadelphia, Arkansas, home of Ouachita Baptist University. Serving as Professor of Religion in the university and pastor of the local church, I strive, sometimes unsuccessfully, to be creative in communicating biblical truths. This Sunday, August 7, 1983, my sermon, "How to Improve Your Serve," is inspired by Jesus' command to serve one another but also by my neighbor Doug Wilson's love of the game of tennis and his friendly tennis tips for his minister-neighbor.

I'm hoping a visual lesson from the pulpit today might improve the homily and help the parishioners remember the points of my message correlating serving in tennis with serving in Christian life. We should

• Concentrate on serving correctly, keeping our eye on the ball (focus).

• Think positively.

• Learn from those who serve better than we (Jesus and the saints).

• Practice, practice, practice.

With my "wisdom" imparted, I reach for a tennis racket and ball from behind the pulpit to deliver an unforgettable lesson on the proper way to serve, which will summarize my sermon points.

Carefully aiming the struck ball to fly off the racket toward Van Barrett, the Ouachita baseball coach sitting beside his wife Julie, I know the athletic coach will catch and return the ball. Instead, having received no advance warning from me, Van's quick reflexes cause him to duck sideways. Sitting directly behind Coach Barrett is our oldest deacon, Mr. Roy Buck, sound asleep! He catches the ball on his forehead! *WOP!* Gasps ricochet around the sanctuary. Mrs. Buck cries out loud, "Honey, are you all right?"

Mr. Buck awakens, rubs his head, and laughs. I, red-faced and shell-shocked, meekly declare, "Church over—and probably my pastorate!"

The Case of the Illegally Cut and Stolen Christmas Tree

Kay and I are enjoying a stroll through our neighborhood in Iowa during the Christmas season when we decide to meander aimlessly through inviting connecting lanes and garden paths. Wandering upon the beautifully manicured grounds of an upscale retirement village some distance from our home, we remark how the breathtaking Christmas scene reminds us of the paintings of Norman Rockwell and Thomas Kinkade.

Then we see it.

Stripped of its crowning eight-foot-tall triangular top, an embarrassed Christmas tree-shaped Scotch pine stands naked before us!

"Look at that!" I say. "Who would do that?"

"Oh, my goodness!" Kay echoes. "How awful! Can you believe it?"

"No, I can't. Vandals! Brazen thieves with saws. Such a shame!"

"Look over there!" Kay points. "Is that the treetop on the back of their property?"

To our surprise, the ill-fated hardwood trophy lies discarded on a damp mulch pile near an adjoining wooded area along the village perimeter. We walk over. "You've got to be kidding me! Who would cut the top out of a tree, then leave it or throw it away like that?"

"Maybe they thought it wasn't pretty enough. Or maybe someone was coming and they fled."

"Yeah, maybe so. Or the staff might have found it and tried to use it in the lobby, but it was too big."

"Yeah, maybe, but I surely don't believe the staff cut it down."

"Oh, heavens no! I don't either. Sad!"

Two days later we are out walking again. Our path leads back to the domain of the rejected evergreen. "Hon, if no one is going to use this tree, I think I'll come get it and put it in our front yard with lights. Give it a good Christmas home."

"You can't do that. It's not yours. You can't just take it."

"Why not? It's just thrown away. It's gonna die and decay."

"I know, but it's not yours. You can't take someone else's property."

"It's not their property. It's their trash. We can give the tree a Christmas home and help the village, too."

"I know you mean well, hon, but you could get in trouble doing that. What if they see you and think you're the culprit returning to the scene of the crime?"

"Yeah, you're right."

The next day, while Kay is away from home, I drive to the mulch pile, secure the large conifer, and then motor proudly into our driveway with my prize. Kay drives in behind me. "Randall, what have you done?"

"Honey, it's okay. It's their trash and our treasure."

"Your treasure, not mine."

"Okay, my treasure. But you'll love it when I get the lights on it."

"I'll bring you fruitcake in jail for Christmas."

Eliciting admiration from our neighbors I'm sure, the elegant tree graces our lawn this Christmas season. Our young grandchildren love it. When neighbor Jim comments on our holiday feature, I proudly boast of my find.

"So, you're the guy?" Jim asks.

"What guy is that?"

"The vandal who cut the top out of the tree at the retirement village?"

"Oh, no, no, no! Like I said, I only found it thrown on a dump."

"Well, I was having coffee with my retired buddies this morning at Panera Bread. Two of them live in the village. Said someone destroyed one of their beautiful trees, cut it up, and made off with its top for a Yuletide evergreen. Was that you?"

"It certainly was not!"

"I believe you, but it's in your yard."

"'Cause they threw it away."

"I believe you, but everyone at the retirement village is upset. They've filed a police report and plan to press charges for destruction of property and theft."

"Oh, this is bad. Kay's gonna kill me."

"Not if the old folks at the village find you first."

Woe is me! What do I do now?

Kay is convinced Santa is coming down our chimney wearing a badge. Maybe. But, at least so far, law enforcement officers have not shown up at our door with a search warrant or a warrant for my arrest. In the event my holiday luck changes, here is the address of the Ames, Iowa, Police Department: 515 Clark Ave, Ames, IA, 50010. In care of Public Enemy Numberless One Randall O'Brien, just send that Christmas fruitcake to my cold cell.

The Weirdest Liquid on Earth

Nothing else comes close. It is by far the weirdest liquid on Earth. Essential for life, it covers 71 percent of the planet's surface. Oceans contain 97 percent of the world's volume. Human bodies are composed of a variable amount, depending on our age; but a general range of 60-70 percent seems fair to declare.

The human brain and heart consist of 73 percent of the compound, lungs 83 percent, muscles and kidney 79 percent, and plasma 90 percent. None of this is what makes water weird. Are you ready for this?

Weird fact #1: Water, or H_2O, as every fourth grader knows to call it, is composed of two hydrogen atoms and 1 oxygen atom per molecule. But think about it. Hydrogen is a highly flammable *gas*. Oxygen is an absolute prerequisite for fire. Every school child knows a glass placed over a lit candle extinguishes the flame as the oxygen expires. Yet, when these two elements, hydrogen and oxygen, are put together in just the right fashion—two parts hydrogen and one part oxygen—the result produces a compound not to cause fire but to put out fire! Who's creating this place?

Weird fact #2: Molecules expand when heated but contract when cooled, correct? Hot air rises and cool air falls, right? Why? Because cold molecules constrict, increasing in density and weight. Becoming heavier, they drop. Hot air, on the other hand, expands, decreasing in density, becoming lighter, and rising.

Water behaves like this, too (as do other liquids). As water cools, it drops to the bottom of the pond, river, lake, ocean, or container.

Up to a point.

Water behaves *exactly* as other liquids . . . *until* it reaches 39.2 degrees Fahrenheit. At this point its molecules, which have been *contracting*, no longer do so. Upon arriving at the temperature of freezing—32 degrees—water molecules begin to *expand*! That's right: not contract but expand.

Instead of becoming denser and heavier, then sinking to the bottom of the body of water, frozen water, or ice, becomes lighter and *floats*. Were ice to behave as *all other liquids*, it would sink to the bottom of our bodies of water. Waterways freezing from bottom to top would bring ecological disaster. Entrapped in ice, marine life would freeze and die. But with ice freezing from the top down, marine life and plant life are covered, insulated, protected, and allowed to carry on beneath the ice.

No other liquid behaves in this manner. Without water's jaw-dropping ways, life on Earth as we know it could not exist. But here we are, thanks to the Master Chemist.

And the weirdest liquid on Earth.

What Kris Learned from His Father

We made the decision to give the local Montessori school an opportunity to help educate our highly active elementary-age son. Group activities, areas for independent trial-and-error learning, multisensory, open floor environment, and development of the whole child seemed to offer the perfect fit for Kris.

Unlike the large Texas public schools our daughters attended, Kris's school was small with fewer students in each class. Teachers knew both their students and their highly invested parents.

Our son's teacher seemed to be particularly pleased to have in her class the son of Baylor University's provost. On several occasions she graciously, even eagerly, made reference to my work at the university.

One fine day, class discussion included a segment that focused on "something your parents taught you." The teacher began the exercise by commenting how important it is for us to learn from our personal experiences, through experimentation, but also from others. She continued, "Today, let's share one thing we learned from our fathers."

The first child the teacher calls on replies, "My daddy taught me to always say the magic words, *please* and *thank you*." The young girl receives the chatty approval of the learning circle. The second student she calls on, a boy, offers, "My daddy taught me how to tie my shoes. And now I can do it all by myself."

"Very good," says the teacher.

"Kris, why don't you share with the class something important you learned from your father, Dr. O'Brien?"

"My daddy taught me it's okay to pee in the shower if you aim for the drain."

Teacher resuscitation successful.

When Dreams Come True

Shannon is a gymnast. Her idols? Kim Zmeskal, Shannon Miller, Kerri Strug, Dominique Dawes, Jaycie Phelps, Dominique Moceanu, and the like. Her dream? To compete in the Olympics, like thousands of other young gymnasts. To represent the USA one day. Ah, sweet dreams.

Shannon is different than all other dreamers. Shannon is the only thirteen-year-old in the universe who happens to be my daughter. Maybe I can't make her dream come true of becoming an Olympic gymnast. But I can surely see to it that she *goes* to the Olympics. Talent and tickets are separate matters.

One year before the 1996 Olympic Games begin in Atlanta, Georgia, we order tickets for the women's gymnastics competition. Our luck? One set of tickets for one morning session only, Tuesday, July 23.

Would you travel 1,800 miles roundtrip for a three-hour tumbling performance by little pixies, none of whom you know? What if the little darlings are the goddesses of your daughter's religion, and Mt. Olympus beckons, where gods and goddesses reveal their glory every four years?

Atlanta, here we come! O'Briens to the Olympics! Decked out in red, white, and blue, 900 miles later, we arrive. So does the bad news. Our tickets, we learn, are not for the American session of gymnastic competition. Try France, Canada, Australia, and Kazakhstan! No

USA. No Shannon Miller. No Kerri Strug. No Dominique Moceanu. No dream come true of seeing idols perform. No happy daughter.

"You girls go on ahead in the Georgia Dome. Mom and I and your brother will catch up with you later."

Big sister Elise and Shannon take off briskly, pacing toward the turnstiles. We dash toward the ticket line.

"Any tickets left for the American gymnastic session?"

"Sorry. Hard sellout."

"What I suspected. Just our luck."

"*Wait*! Who is that? What's that man holding up over there? What's he selling? Hon, you don't think . . . ?"

"I don't know."

"Hey you! Mister! Wait up! Whatcha got? Wouldn't happen to have tickets for the afternoon American gymnastics competition, would you?"

"Got two. Want 'em?"

"How much?"

"A buck-fifty apiece."

"You mean . . . ?"

"That's right. $150 each."

"I'll take both."

Folks remember different things about the '96 Atlanta Olympics, I'm sure. Some surely remember Michael Johnson winning the gold medal in both the 200 and 400 meters, a first in Olympic track history, or his World Record time in the 200 meters. Others may recall Carl Lewis winning his fourth consecutive gold medal in the long jump. Many will never forget the bomb planted in Olympic Park. Millions witnessed Kerri Strug, despite torn ankle ligaments, vault into our hearts to secure the first gold medal ever for the American gymnastic team, "The Magnificent Seven."

I'll remember those things, too. But none of those memories hold first place in my heart. Unless you're a parent, you might not understand, but I bet you will. My most unforgettable moment—hands down—my *personal* gold medal memory? Handing those two tickets to Shannon and Elise.

"Mother and Daddy have something for you girls. Here you go; we love you."

"Yiiiiiiiiiiiiiiieeeeeeeeeeee!!! Dad, *where did you get these?!* Oh, my gosh!! Dad, you're the GREATEST!"

Whose dream came true?

www.ingramcontent.com/pod-product-compliance
Lightning Source LLC
LaVergne TN
LVHW050628100826
845148LV00011B/1778

* 9 7 8 1 6 4 1 7 3 3 3 2 8 *